MUSIC THEORY FOR KIDS

AN ILLUSTRATED GUIDE FOR HEROIC BEGINNERS

BY KIT MASSEY

To access additional worksheets visit:
www.halleonard.com/mylibrary

1842-3705-6127-4643

ISBN 979-835011633-5

HAL•LEONARD®

Visit Hal Leonard Online at **www.halleonard.com**

Explore the entire family of Hal Leonard products and resources

World headquarters, contact:
Hal Leonard
7777 West Bluemound Road
Milwaukee, WI 53213
Email: info@halleonard.com

In Europe, contact:
Hal Leonard Europe Limited
Dettingen Way
Bury St Edmunds, Suffolk, IP33 3YB
Email: info@halleonardeurope.com

In Australia, contact:
Hal Leonard Australia Pty. Ltd.
4 Lentara Court
Cheltenham, Victoria, 3192 Australia
Email: info@halleonard.com.au

INTRODUCTION

WHY? WHY HAVE I BEEN MADE TO DO MUSIC THEORY?

That's a great question. But to answer it, we need to understand what music theory actually is. Music theory is how music is written down. Writing music down is one way of communicating our ideas to each other and passing them on.

WHY BOTHER WRITING MUSIC DOWN? I LIKE PLAYING AND LISTENING TO MUSIC.

MUSIC THEORY IS LIKE A SET OF TOOLS.

Think of stories. We can tell stories to one another that we've learnt by heart. But some stories are too long to do this accurately. So, we write them down and then everyone can read them. But in order to read and write, we need to learn the alphabet, phonics, how to spell, and how grammar works. If we want to read and write music, we also need to learn the alphabet and the grammar of music. And that's where music theory comes in.

We can use tools to take things apart. We can use music theory to take music apart and see how it's put together. This will help us to understand more about the story that the music is telling.

We can use tools to build things. We can use music theory to write down our own pieces. The more we understand about the way music works, the more ideas we'll have!

SO, MUSIC THEORY ENABLES US TO BETTER UNDERSTAND THE MUSIC WE LISTEN TO AND THE MUSIC THAT WE PLAY. IT HELPS US COME UP WITH OUR OWN IDEAS, TOO. AND IT ALLOWS US TO SHARE MUSIC WITH OTHERS.

THIS BOOK BELONGS TO:	
MY MUSICAL INSTRUMENT IS:	
MY FAVOURITE KIND OF PIZZA IS:	

PEOPLE TO LOOK OUT FOR

Mr Crotchety

Mr Crotchety, the school music teacher, can be a little strict but he really just wants the pupils to be the best they can be.

Billy

Billy plays drums in the school orchestra. He loves playing loudly. His neighbour (the pizza chef, Alfonzo) is less keen.

Cecil

Cecil is the clumsiest flute player you will ever meet. He's lost his music. Again.

Hayley

Hayley is the school's best tuba player. She takes care of all the low notes in the music.

The Masked Composer

You'll get some great tips from this person along the way. But who is this musical hero?

THINGS TO LOOK OUT FOR

MY THEORY SCRAPBOOK

We're going on a journey together. At the end of each chapter, you'll see a scrapbook with all the important memories from your learning. Go back over these if you need to.

HOW DO I FEEL?

At the end of each chapter, you'll have the chance to reflect on how you are feeling about the work you have just done. Be honest. There are extra, downloadable resources if you require a bit of help. And always ask a teacher or another adult if you get stuck.

YOU BE THE COMPOSER

Every chapter will give you the chance to write your own music. This will bring the theory to life, helping you to apply what you've learnt and create new music that is yours. Be creative!

MORE THAN THIS BOOK

We all need a bit of extra help from time to time. If required, you can access additional PDF activities to consolidate your learning. Simply look for the ⬇ Download icon, go to **www.halleonard.com/mylibrary**, and enter the code found on page 1.

CONTENTS

CHAPTER 1
SAVE BILLY. EAT PIZZA.

MUSICAL TOPICS
The beat, note values, bars, bar lines, and time signatures ($\frac{4}{4}$, $\frac{2}{4}$).

THE BEAT

This is Billy. Billy loves pizza. He also loves playing in his school orchestra. But today Billy is pretty worried. He's lost his music and the rehearsal is in 20 minutes.

Don't worry, Billy, we're going to write you a part! First, we need to know a few things about how music is written down.

Most music has a steady **BEAT**, a bit like your heartbeat or the steady ticking of a clock. You know when you clap along to a piece of music? That's the beat you're clapping!

Put your fingers on your wrist. Can you feel your pulse?

Congratulations!

You're definitely NOT a vampire. Hopefully.

A note that lasts one beat looks like this. It's called a **CROTCHET**.

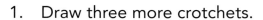

1. Draw three more crotchets.

GREAT DRAWING!
It's good that we've got four crotchets because music usually works in fours.

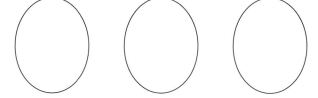

MARCHING IN FOUR

Up on your feet. Let me see those toes!

You march like this:

1,2,3,4   **1**,2,3,4

The first step is the heaviest.

Left, right, left, right   **Left**, right, left, right

NOTE VALUES

At ease! The term **NOTE VALUE** means how long a note lasts. Here are some note values to get to know.

NOTE SYMBOL	NOTE NAME	LASTS FOR... (VALUE)	LOOKS LIKE A...
𝅝	Semibreve	Four Beats	Doughnut
𝅗𝅥	Minim	Two Beats	Doughnut with an antenna
♩	Crotchet	One Beat	Daddy long-legs with only one leg
♪	Quaver	Half a Beat	Tomato with a broken antenna

2. **QUICKFIRE QUIZ.** Use the note-value table to help you with these questions. (Write lightly with a pencil, check your answers, and then rub them out.) Then, after taking a break, go back and do them again, without peeking at the table at all!

a.) What's the name of this note value? 𝅝 _____

b.) Draw the note value that lasts for two beats. _____

c.) If you are doing this for a second time, stop peeking at the note-value table.

d.) Draw a quaver. _____

e.) What does a crotchet look like? _____

f.) For how long does a quaver last? _____

g.) Draw a circle around the shortest note value.

h.) Draw a circle around the longest note value.

WHAT'S THE MOST MUSICAL PART OF YOUR BODY?

YOUR NOSE. YOU CAN BLOW AND PICK IT!

DAD JOKE CORNER

COUNTING

Everyone loves maths, right? I knew you'd agree! Let's do some musical maths.

$$\quad + \quad = \quad \text{2 beats}$$

(1 beat) + (1 beat)

3. How many beats do these note values add up to?

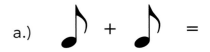

a.) ♪ + ♪ =

b.) 𝅝 + ♩ =

c.) ♩ + 𝅗𝅥 =

d.) 𝅝 + ♩ + 𝅗𝅥 =

e.) 𝅗𝅥 + ♩ + 𝅗𝅥 =

A group of note values that form a pattern is called a *RHYTHM*. Here's a useful way of remembering how to spell it.

R	H	Y	T	H	M
H	E	O	W	I	O
Y	L	U	O	P	V
T	P	R		S	E
H	S				
M					

CLASSIC DAD DANCING

Quavers are the friendliest of notes and often like to go around in pairs.
When you see them in this way, they make up one beat. (Two sounds to one beat.)

Note values all belong to a sort of musical family tree. It shows us how all the note values relate to each other. Wow, that semibreve has a lot of descendants!

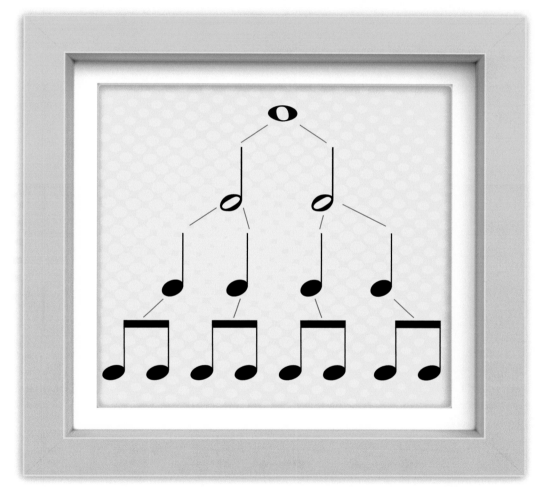

4. Draw two note values that add up to the notes below.

a.) ♩ = _____ + _____

b.) o = _____ + _____

c.) ♩ = _____ + _____

BARS AND BAR LINES

THIS IS A SNARE DRUM.

Drumhead, made from plastic or animal skin

Drumsticks

Body, made from wood or brass

Drum snares (pieces of wire that make the drum rattle)

COMPOSE YOURSELF

Billy's school has been practising a piece with a strong beat called the *Radetzky March*. Why not go online and listen to it? It was written by a guy called Johann Strauss I (1804–1849). He had a son, also called Johann. Imaginative. Johann "senior" was so jealous of his son's musical ability that he actually tried to ruin his career. And you thought adults were bad for making you tidy up!

Billy's snare-drum part has a rhythm that repeats over and over. A repeated musical pattern is called an *OSTINATO*.

Here's the rhythm.

5. Billy has been told to write the music out three more times; Mr Crotchety says it'll help Billy learn how to play it. Go on, be a good friend and do it for him! (The first note value has been done for you.)

a.) _____

b.) _____

c.) _____

It's easier to understand beats and note values when we count them aloud. This is called saying the **BEAT COUNT**. Let's practise the beat count first for crotchets. Read the music and clap the crotchets while saying the beat count aloud. (The beat count is represented by numbers under the notes.) Keep the beat steady in each counting exercise.

Now, let's do the same thing with minims.

Finally, let's do it again with semibreves.

When we count quavers, we say, "one–and–two–and–three–and–four–and." Let's practise that together, clapping and counting.

You are now able to clap and count the ostinato from earlier!

These vertical lines are called **BAR LINES**. They split the music up into groups of beats. Bar lines make music easier to read.

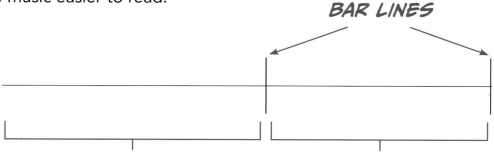

Each group is called a **BAR**.

(Imagineifwedidn'tbothertoputspacesbetweenwords. That's a bit like reading music without bar lines and bars.)

These two lines are called a *DOUBLE BAR LINE*. Music is often organised into sections such as an introduction, verse, or chorus. To show when a section ends, we use a double bar line. In this book, our short musical exercises will end with this symbol.

DOUBLE BAR LINE

These two dark lines make up the *FINAL BAR LINE*. These are used at the very end of a piece of music. It's a bit like when you see "THE END" written on the last page of a book.

FINAL BAR LINE

All of these symbols make it easier for us to read the music on the page.

6. How many beats in a bar does Billy's snare-drum ostinato have? _____

7. Split the following music up into bars of four beats with bar lines.

TIME SIGNATURES

Before playing a piece, a musician could work out how many beats are in a bar by counting through all the music. But performers are busy people. They don't have time to waste working out stuff like that! So, to tell them how many beats are in each bar, musicians are given a symbol at the beginning of a piece of music called a *TIME SIGNATURE*. Neat, huh?

4 ← This tells us there are four beats in each bar.

4 ← This bottom number is a code! The "4" stands for "crotchet."
It means a beat is worth one crotchet. So, here there are four crotchet beats in each bar.

HERE'S ANOTHER TIME SIGNATURE!

2 ← This tells us there are two beats in each bar.

4 ← Remember, the "4" stands for "crotchet." It means a crotchet is worth one beat. So, two crotchet beats in each bar.

8. Add the correct time signature to each of these bars.

9. These extracts have missing note values. Add one note value to make sure that the bars have the right number of beats.

YOU BE THE COMPOSER!

An author is someone who writes a book. A composer is someone who creates a piece of music. Sometimes, they write the music down so that other people can play it. Music that is written down is called *SHEET MUSIC*. You don't have to have cool hair to be a composer. But it does help.

10. Write a two-bar rhythm piece for Billy to play. Include the time signature and a bar line. It doesn't have to be an ostinato. Every bar can have a different rhythm!

TIP FROM THE MASKED COMPOSER!

MAKE SURE THAT THERE ARE THE CORRECT NUMBER OF BEATS IN EVERY BAR BY SAYING THE BEAT COUNT. YOU CAN MAKE YOUR PIECE OF MUSIC INTERESTING BY CHOOSING A VARIETY OF NOTE VALUES. BUT KEEP YOUR QUAVERS HOLDING HANDS IN PAIRS.

HOW DO I FEEL?

We've learnt about the *BEAT*, *NOTE VALUES*, *BARS*, *BAR LINES*, and *TIME SIGNATURES*. How did you do with this chapter?

Yes, I understand all of this.	🙂	Why don't you extend the rhythm you wrote for Billy to four bars, using a greater mixture of note values?
I think I understand but some bits were tricky.	😐	Great job for realising this. Look through the notes again and ask your teacher about the tricky bits.
I still don't understand most of it.	🙁	Hey, all of us struggle sometimes. Go over from the beginning with your teacher or another adult. To get some extra help, download more worksheet exercises, here. 

MY THEORY SCRAPBOOK

Sheet Music: Music that is written down.

Composer: A person who creates a piece of music.

Beat: The regular pulse in music that we tap or clap.

Beat Count: The verbalisation of the beat. (Counting the beat aloud.)

Semibreve o: A note value worth four beats.

Minim ♩: A note value worth two beats.

Crotchet ♩: A note value worth one beat.

Quaver ♪: A note value worth half a beat.

Bar Line: A line that divides written music into units called bars.

Bar: The space in between bar lines where musical notes are written.

Double Bar Line: Two bar lines next to each other, showing the end of a section or example of music.

Final Bar Line: A set of two, thick bar lines showing the end of a piece of music.

Time Signature: The two numbers at the start of sheet music that tell us how many beats are in a bar.

Ostinato: A repeated musical pattern.

$\frac{4}{4}$: A time signature showing there are four crotchet beats in each bar.

$\frac{2}{4}$: A time signature showing there are two crotchet beats in each bar.

Antelope: An ant with a runaway bride.

CHAPTER 2
THE SCHOOL ORCHESTRA

MUSICAL TOPICS

The stave, the musical alphabet, noteheads and stems, clefs, note names, and the grand staff.

This is Cecil.

Cecil is in the school orchestra. His dog ate his sheet music and he's very worried. Mr Crotchety is going to hit the roof! Don't worry, Cecil, we'll write you some flute music that will fit with the rest of the orchestra perfectly. Mr Crotchety will never even know!

THE STAVE

Writing sheet music helps us remember music and play it to other people. (Just like writing stories means we can remember our ideas and share them!) Billy's drum music was written on one line, but a lot of music is written on what we call a *STAVE*.

It has five lines and looks a bit like telegraph wires.

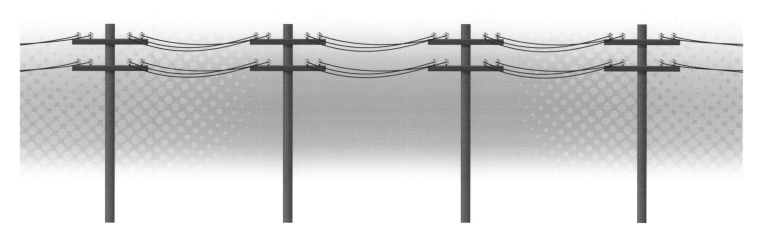

Musical notes are represented on the stave by blobs called **NOTEHEADS**. They can be on the lines, like this.

1. Draw some noteheads on the lines.

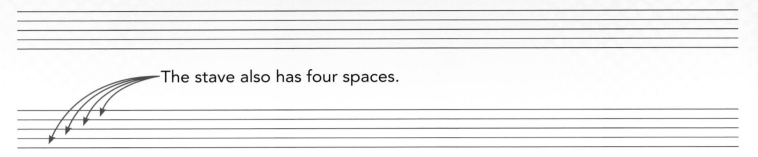

The stave also has four spaces.

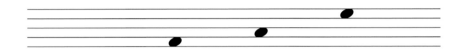

Noteheads can also be in the spaces of the stave, like this.

2. Draw some noteheads in the spaces.

You can think of noteheads like birds that are either sitting on a telegraph wire or flying between the spaces.

Here's a stave with some of the symbols we have learnt so far. Draw a line connecting the term to the correct symbol.

Double Bar Line   Notehead

Bar   Bar Line

CLEFS

The *PITCH* of a note means how high or low it is.

You can think of the stave as like a ladder. The higher a notehead is on the stave, the higher its pitch.

Instruments that play high pitches use a symbol at the beginning of the music called a *TREBLE CLEF*. (Music written for a piano player's right hand also uses the treble clef.)

3. Draw some more treble clefs. Begin by joining the dots for your first go, starting at the centre of the clef. Then, do the rest freehand.

Instruments that are lower in pitch use a symbol at the beginning of the music called a *BASS CLEF*. (Music written for a piano player's left hand also uses the bass clef.)

4. Draw some more bass clefs. Begin by joining the dots for your first go, starting at the curve on the top-left. Then, do the rest freehand.

5. Here are some instruments from the school orchestra. Can you guess which ones use the treble clef and which ones use the bass clef? Draw a line between the instrument and the clef it uses.

Trombone **Violin** **Flute** **Double Bass**

TIP FROM THE MASKED COMPOSER!

HERE'S A CLUE.

MOST OF THE TIME,
THE BIGGER THE INSTRUMENT,
THE LOWER THE SOUND.

THE MUSICAL ALPHABET

Did you know that notes are named after letters of the alphabet? WHAT?! OK, it's not that dramatic. This alphabet of music is called—wait for it—the *MUSICAL ALPHABET*!

Even if you don't play the piano, looking at a piano keyboard is an easy way of visualising the notes.

This pattern of notes repeats again and again as you go further up the piano keyboard. If you can, find and play these notes on a piano, keyboard, piano app, or pitched percussion.

Oh, no! Cecil has spilled something disgusting on his piano keyboard. (Classic Cecil.) Urgh, what on earth IS that? Let's try not think about it. Instead, write in the letter names for the keys that have been splashed with the gross stuff.

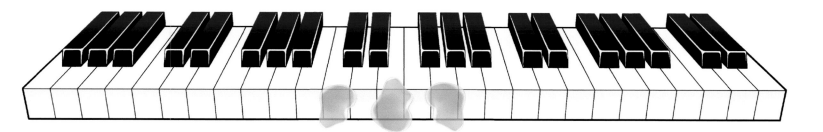

We use the letters "A–G" to label musical notes. But instead of carrying on to "H," we just go back to "A" again.

THE GRAND STAFF

The **GRAND STAFF** is used in sheet music written for the piano. It's basically one big stave with the treble and bass clef on it! Here is a grand staff with notes (labelled) on the lines and spaces.

It's the clef that gives each notehead its name. As you can see, the lines and spaces have different names when we use the treble clef and when we use the bass clef.

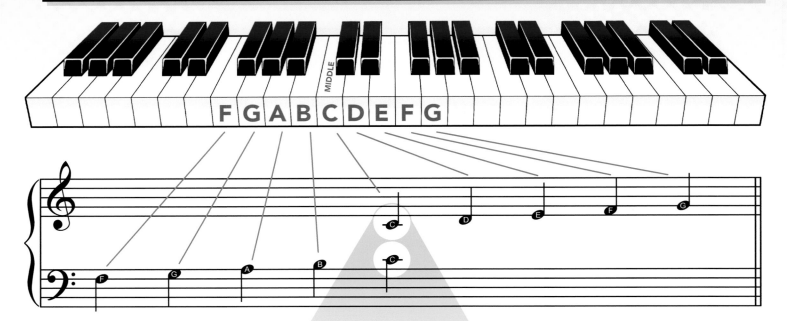

Both of these notes sound the same. They are called **MIDDLE C**.
Think of them as non-identical twins. They sound the same but, on paper, they look different.

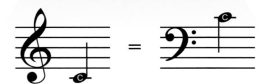

Because they're outside of the stave, they have their own
special little line running through them called a **LEDGER LINE**.

Can you see that noteheads almost always have stems?
Here, in the treble clef, the stems go up (like a tomato with a snorkel).

In the bass clef, the stems go down (like a balloon on a string).

6. Add the stems to these treble-clef noteheads. Make all the stems go up. Then, circle the highest pitch.

7. a.) Add the stems to these bass-clef noteheads. Make all the stems go down. Then, circle the lowest pitch.

b.) Now, add the correct letter name underneath each treble-clef note. Use the grand-staff diagram to help.

_____   _____   _____   _____   _____

c.) Finally, add the correct letter name underneath each bass-clef note. Use the grand-staff diagram to help.

_____   _____   _____   _____   _____

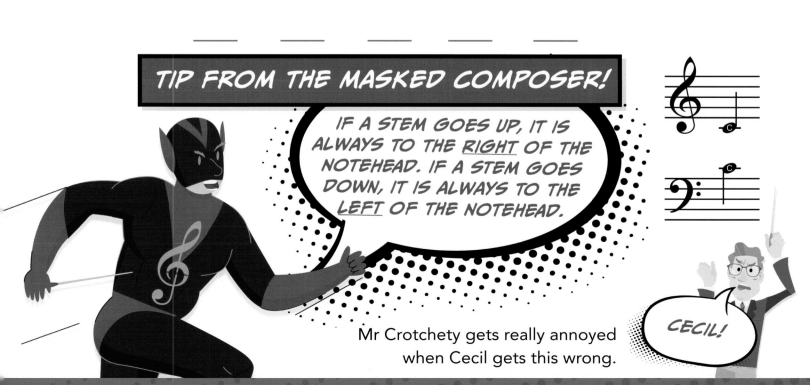

TIP FROM THE MASKED COMPOSER!

IF A STEM GOES UP, IT IS ALWAYS TO THE RIGHT OF THE NOTEHEAD. IF A STEM GOES DOWN, IT IS ALWAYS TO THE LEFT OF THE NOTEHEAD.

Mr Crotchety gets really annoyed when Cecil gets this wrong.

CECIL!

Here's a stave with some of the symbols we have learnt so far. Draw a line connecting the term to the correct symbol.

Treble Clef **Stem** **Notehead**

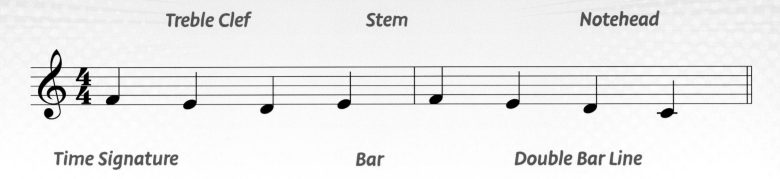

Time Signature **Bar** **Double Bar Line**

THE TREBLE CLEF

Remember, we now know five notes in the treble clef.

Here's what Cecil's sheet music looked like before the dog ate it.

8. Draw an arrow on Cecil's sheet music to each of the following.

"C" Crotchet **"G" Minim** **"C" Semibreve**

"D" Quaver **Bar Line** **Time Signature** **Final Bar Line**

9. Maybe you'd like to try and play this on your instrument? Here's what Cecil's music looks like now…

Have a closer look at Cecil's music.
If you look carefully, you'll see that the time signature is written **after** the clef.
(The time signature will also only appear once, on the first line of music.)

THE BASS CLEF

Remember, we now know five notes in the bass clef.

Hayley is the school's best tuba player. She plays all the low notes and reads the bass clef.

10. Mr Crotchety is shouting out notes for Hayley to play. Help her out by writing them down.

FOUR CROTCHETS: C, F, G, AND B. THEN, ONE SEMIBREVE: A!

11. Cecil has had a go at writing out some new music. Mr Crotchety is not impressed. Can you spot **six** mistakes that Cecil has made in his treble-clef melody? Draw a ring around each one.

Give Cecil a grade and draw an emoji that shows the quality of his work.

SAY WHAT?!
The literal translation of the Japanese word karaoke is "empty orchestra."

YOU BE THE COMPOSER!

12. Now, it's your turn! Compose four bars of music for Cecil to play with the orchestra. Use any of the notes from middle C–G, with a good mix of quavers, crotchets, minims, and semibreves. Remember, we write music on the stave from left to right!

TIP FROM THE MASKED COMPOSER!

STARTING AND ENDING YOUR PIECE ON THE NOTE "C" GIVES IT A STRONG BEGINNING AND MAKES IT SOUND PROPERLY FINISHED, TOO.

13. Play your melody a few times in a row and turn it into an ostinato.

COMPOSE YOURSELF

The composer Chiquinha Gonzaga was the first ever recognised female conductor in Brazil. Now, there's someone who knew her time signatures! As well as being an awesome musician, she also formed the first society in Brazil to enable copyright protection on music. Oh, and she has her own Google Doodle. (Enough said.)

HOW DO I FEEL?

We've learnt about the *STAVE*, *CLEFS*, and *PITCH*. How did you do with this chapter?

Yes, I understand all of this.	🙂	On some manuscript paper, write out a tune in the bass clef for Hayley to play, too.
I think I understand but some bits were tricky.	😐	Great job for realising this. Look through the notes again and ask your teacher about the tricky bits.
I still don't understand most of it.	🙁	Hey, all of us struggle sometimes. Go over from the beginning with your teacher or another adult. To get some extra help, download more worksheet exercises, here. 

MY THEORY SCRAPBOOK

Stave: The five lines and four spaces that music is written down on.

Notehead: An oval-shaped symbol representing a musical note on the stave.

Stem: The vertical line attached to a notehead.

Pitch: High and low musical sounds.

Treble Clef: The symbol on the stave used by high-sounding instruments. It determines the names of the notes on the stave.

Bass Clef: The symbol on the stave used by low-sounding instruments. It determines the names of the notes on the stave.

Musical Alphabet: The pattern of note names in music, going from A–G.

Grand Staff: The stave that includes both treble and bass clefs together, one under another. Used for piano sheet music.

Ledger Lines: Small stave lines drawn onto noteheads that are higher or lower than the stave.

Crookodile: A thieving alligator.

CHAPTER 3
MUSIC FOR SPIES

MUSICAL TOPICS

Steps and skips, more treble and bass notes, dynamics, and tempo.

WELL DONE, COMPOSER! You've written two pieces, so now it's time for our first commission. A commission is when someone asks a composer to write a piece of music for a particular reason.

Who's that? It's only famous film director, Adagietta Maestra!

RING! RING!

DARLING! I'D LOVE FOR YOU TO COMPOSE SOME MUSIC FOR MY NEW FILM. IT'S ALL ABOUT SPIES: SNEAKING ABOUT, FOLLOWING PEOPLE, FALLING DOWN TRAP DOORS. (THAT SORT OF THING.) I JUST KNOW YOU'RE GOING TO DO A FANTASTIC JOB. CIAO, DARLING!

What character of music is going to fit a film about spies? Sneaky music, maybe? Really high, tip-toeing music? Quiet with sudden loud bits?

1. Write down some ideas of what spy music could sound like on a scrap piece of paper.

- Sneaky music
- Really high, tip-toeing music

Don't worry if you get stuck along the way. Cecil and Hayley are around to help out.

First, we're going to need to learn some **more notes** so that they can play extra high in the treble clef and extra low in the bass clef. This will give our film music the impact it needs.

We'll also learn some musical expressions to make the music sound exciting and colourful.

NEW NOTES FOR THE TREBLE CLEF

Here are some more notes for Cecil to play in the treble clef. They get higher and higher!

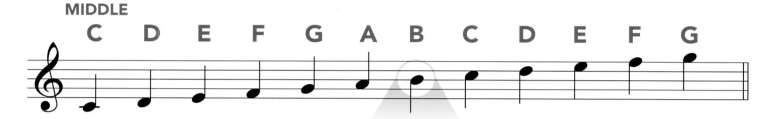

MIDDLE
C D E F G A B C D E F G

Notice that the stems on the notes in the lower half of the stave go up and those in the upper half of the stave go down. The note on the middle line can go either way!

2. Cecil is trying to play some higher notes on his flute. Give him some help by writing in the names of the notes.

Can you play the notes on your instrument?

3. Cecil and Billy are playing a short *DUET*. A duet is a piece for two musicians. They are playing in *RHYTHMIC UNISON*. This means that they are playing exactly the same rhythm. Add the rest of the notes for Cecil's part, matching Billy's rhythm. The note names are written underneath Cecil's treble-clef stave. Red arrows show whether the next note is higher or lower than the one before.

This is called a *PERCUSSION CLEF*. It's used for some percussion instruments that don't play musical pitches.

↑↓D ↓A A   ↓G   ↑↓B   ↑C ↓G↓E ↓middle C

STEPS AND SKIPS

When notes move between a line and a space, we say they are moving by *STEP*. You might use this kind of tune in the film when a spy is climbing up a rope ladder.

STEP

When notes move between a line and a line, or a space and a space, we say they are moving by *SKIPS*. You might use this kind of tune when a spy is jumping from rooftop to rooftop.

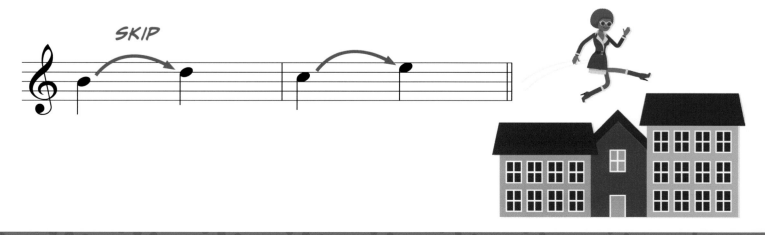

SKIP

4. Here is another one of Cecil's favourite tunes. Draw a straight arrow ➞ between notes that are a step away and a curved arrow ⌒ between notes that are a skip away. Then, write the note names in the squares below.

Can you play this on your instrument?

5. Follow the instructions below and write the correct crotchet note under each question mark.

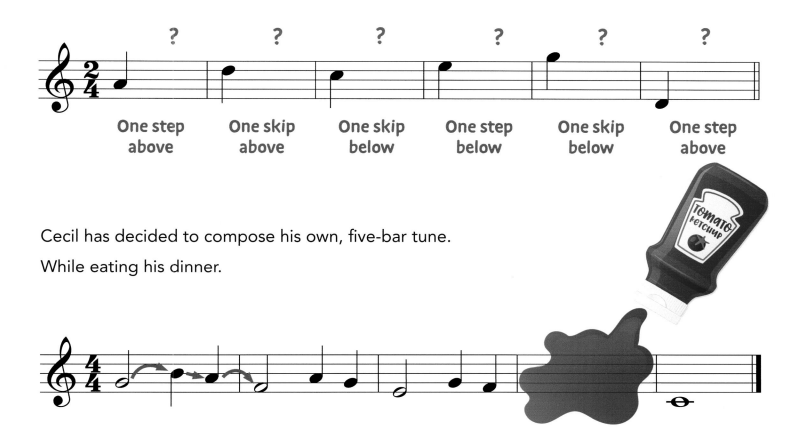

?	?	?	?	?	?
One step above	One skip above	One skip below	One step below	One skip below	One step above

Cecil has decided to compose his own, five-bar tune.

While eating his dinner.

A tune that is repeated up or down in pitch is called a **SEQUENCE**. Can you work out the pattern in the music and guess which notes come in the "ketchup-y" bar? Write out the complete music on the stave below.

NEW NOTES FOR THE BASS CLEF

Here are some more notes for Hayley to play in the bass clef. How low can she go? The notes we've already learnt are in pink. The new notes are in blue.

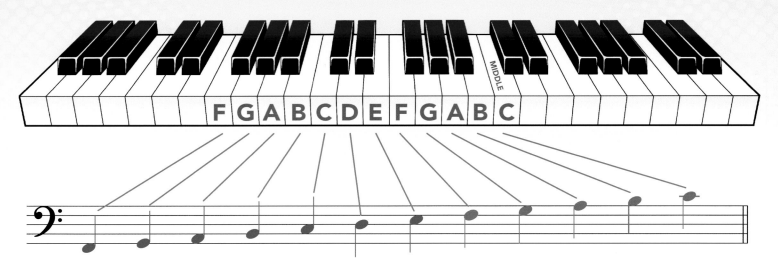

6. It's late at night. Hayley is practising some lovely, low notes. Her neighbours are so happy about this.

Write the lowest version of each note on the stave without using ledger lines. Hayley has written in the first one for you.

a.) "F" semibreve

b.) "A" minim

c.) "C" semibreve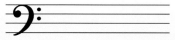

d.) "D" crotchet

e.) "B" quaver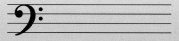

f.) "E" minim

7. Uh-oh, some of Cecil's ketchup has got onto Hayley's music. That flautist is honestly a disaster. But wait, incredibly it seems to have formed a tune! Make each ketchup-notehead a crotchet by giving it a stem going in the correct direction. Then, write the name of the note in the box below.

Finish off the ketchup piece by writing four crotchet notes of your choice per blank bar.

LINES AND SPACES

Some people like to remember the names of the notes by learning a special phrase. These are called **MNEMONICS**. You might have done these at school to help you learn tricky spellings.

The lines in the treble clef spell out the phrase:

Every **G**ood **B**adger **D**eserves **F**udge!

The spaces in the treble clef spell out the word:

F A C E

The lines in the bass clef spell out the phrase:

Grizzly **B**ears **D**on't **F**righten **A**nyone

8. Here are the remaining notes that belong in the spaces of the bass stave. Add the letter names underneath. Can you come up with a memorable phrase that uses the letters?

Draw a picture in the box to illustrate it.

My Drawing

NOTE GAMES

9. Cecil and Hayley are playing the same notes at different pitches. Work out the names of the notes and connect the matching treble and bass staves.

10. Work out the names of the notes and draw a line connecting the stave to its matching image.

11. Adagietta Maestra has some ideas for her film. Can you read this spy story by working out the musical notes?

MUSICAL CODES

Just like spies, we can make secret codes from music.

Many composers love to do this. Some have even hidden their names inside their music, like this guy called Johann Sebastian Bach who lived from 1685–1750! That was AGES ago.

One way of making musical codes is to use a super-secret table like this one.

Every letter in this column uses the note "A."

Every letter in this column uses the note "B," etc. You get the idea!

A	B	C	D	E	F	G
H	I	J	K	L	M	N
O	P	Q	R	S	T	U
V	W	X	Y	Z		

Cecil's name would sound like this in the musical code.

12. Write out your own first name in musical code! Don't worry about stems. Just use noteheads, like Cecil.

Important tunes in a piece of music, such as when you write your name in code like this, are called **THEMES**. So, now that you've got the notes let's use some rhythms to turn it into a theme!

Here is Cecil's theme with some rhythms that he's made up.

13. Now, add some rhythms to your theme. You can use semibreves, mimims, crotchets, and quavers in any order you like. Just make sure there are four beats in every bar.

MY NAME THEME

MUSICAL EXPRESSIONS

In music, we use words to describe how we want the music to be performed (for example, loudly or slowly). A lot of these are in Italian. **"WHY?!"** (You ask.) Well, in the past the Italian language was very fashionable with western composers. To be fair, it is also a very beautiful, musical-sounding language! In any case, learning new languages is amazing; it helps us communicate better to more people.

DYNAMICS describe how loud or soft a piece of music is. Here are some commonly used expressions.

Italian Word	Musical Symbol	English Word
Forte	f	Loud
Fortissimo	$f\!f$	Very Loud
Mezzo Forte	mf	Moderately Loud
Mezzo Piano	mp	Moderately Soft
Piano	p	Soft
Pianissimo	pp	Very Soft
Crescendo (*cresc.*)	◁	Gradually Getting Louder
Diminuendo (*dim.*)	▷	Gradually Getting Softer
Decrescendo (*decresc.*)	▷	Gradually Getting Softer

14. Arrange these dynamics in the box below from quietest to loudest.

$$mf \qquad p \qquad f \qquad mp \qquad pp \qquad f\!f$$

TEMPO is what we call the "speed" of a piece of music.
Here are some commonly used expressions.

Italian Word	English Word	Italian Word	English Word
Adagio	Slow	Rallentando (*rall.*)	Gradually Getting Slower
Lento	Slow	Ritardando (*rit.*)	Gradually Getting Slower
Andante	At a Walking Speed	Ritenuto (*rit.*)	Held Back
Moderato	Moderately	Accelerando (*accel.*)	Gradually Getting Faster
Allegretto	Fairly Fast	Poco	A Little
Allegro	Fast and Lively	Mezzo	Half/Medium/Somewhat

♩ = 132

This is a tempo marking. It means there are 132 crotchet beats a minute. We can use this device, called a metronome, to sound the beat. Sometimes metronomes look like the one in the picture, but you can also access them online or as phone apps. Either way, they can help us to play in time.

15. Alfonzo the Italian chef is yelling at his waiters. When he gets angry, he sometimes uses Italian words. Can you translate what he's saying?

You guys are soooo *LENTO!* You're serving pizza *ANDANTE* and *RALLENTANDO.* You'd better *ACCELERANDO* and start moving *ALLEGRO* or there's going to be trouble! If you think I'm yelling *MEZZO FORTE* now, wait until you hear my *FORTISSIMO!*

16. Describe the expression of this short piece of music by filling in the missing words below (in English).

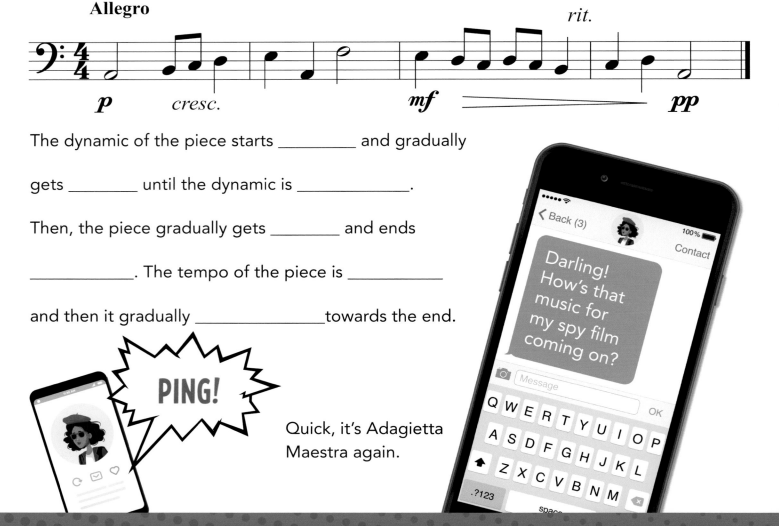

The dynamic of the piece starts _____ and gradually

gets _____ until the dynamic is _____.

Then, the piece gradually gets _____ and ends

_____. The tempo of the piece is _____

and then it gradually _____towards the end.

PING!

Quick, it's Adagietta Maestra again.

Darling! How's that music for my spy film coming on?

17. Whoops, we nearly forgot! Write down some musical expressions on the clipboard that might be useful for your spy piece.

Useful Musical Expressions

SAY WHAT?!

The composer J.S. Bach had 20 children! And a lot of his sheet music got made into jam-jar wrappers when his old house became a jam factory.

WHAT TYPE OF MUSIC ARE BALLOONS AFRAID OF?

POP MUSIC!

DAD JOKE CORNER

YOU BE THE COMPOSER!

18. It's your turn! Compose four bars of music for Adagietta Maestra's spy film. You can use any of the notes we've looked at in this chapter. Which clef to use is up to you!

TIP FROM THE MASKED COMPOSER!

TRY USING MOSTLY STEPS, A FEW SKIPS, AND LOTS OF MUSICAL EXPRESSIONS. GOOD LUCK!

COMPOSE YOURSELF

Need a good role model? Amy Beach was a genius from America who composed music in the late nineteenth century and into the twentieth century. She was a child prodigy. (Meaning, she was better at music as a little kid than pretty much all the adults.) And she had to battle her whole life against a society that didn't approve of women pursuing careers in the arts. In spite of this she wrote a lot of terrific music, one of which is recorded as being the first of its kind by an American woman to have been published. The lesson to learn from Amy Beach? You can do it!

HOW DO I FEEL?

Phew, writing spy music is hard work. Imagine actually being one! We learnt about *STEPS* and *SKIPS, NOTE NAMES, MELODY WRITING, DYNAMICS*, and *TEMPO*. How did you do with this chapter?

Yes, I understand all of this.	🙂	Why not write a new spy piece using a different clef?
I think I understand but some bits were tricky.	😐	Great job for realising this. Look through the notes again and ask your teacher about the tricky bits.
I still don't understand most of it.	🙁	Hey, all of us struggle sometimes. Go over from the beginning with your teacher or another adult. To get some extra help, download more worksheet exercises, here. 

MY THEORY SCRAPBOOK

Rhythmic Unison: Where two or more people perform different parts of music that have exactly the same rhythm.

Step: The movement of one note to another note that is immediately above or beneath it.

Skip: The movement of one note to another note that is greater than a step.

Percussion Clef: A type of clef used for some percussion instruments that can't play pitches.

Sequence: A melodic device that repeats a pattern of notes at a different pitch.

Duet: A piece of music composed for two musicians to play.

Theme: An important tune in a piece of music.

Dynamic: The loudness or softness of music.

Tempo: The speed of a piece of music.

Metronome: A device or app that uses sound to show the tempo of a piece.

Tempo Marking: A marking at the top of sheet music that tells us the exact "beats per minute."

Gummybear: A bear with no teeth.

CHAPTER 4
WALTZING ON ICE

MUSICAL TOPICS

$\frac{3}{4}$ time signature, dotted minim and dotted crotchet, ties, articulation, and features of melody.

Good job, composer! Put your feet up, relax, and have a chocolate brownie. Or an apple. Whichever you prefer.

Wait, hold on! You've just had a message from world-famous ballet dancer, Rodolpho Tutu!

Dearest Amazing Composer,

I heard the music you wrote for Adagietta's spy film. It was magnificent! I simply must have you write some music for a scene in my ballet.

It's a waltz—wait for it—on ice! Can't wait to hear your tune.

Break a leg (not literally),
Rodolpho

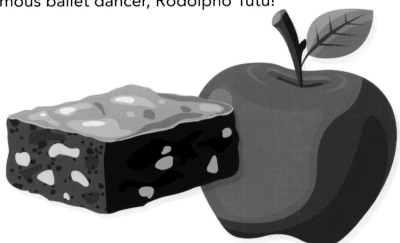

Let's do it! We can have the brownie after. (Or apple.)

Before we're ready to add our waltz music to Rodolpho's ballet, we need to learn a few more things about music theory.

But first, we're going need to learn how to waltz!

THE WALTZ

Some music has three beats per bar. The waltz is one of the most famous types of dance; music for waltzes has three beats per bar.

3 ← Remember, the "3" means that there are three beats in a bar.
4 ← The "4" means that a beat is worth one crotchet.

WALTZING IN THREE

Up on your feet! Or there's no chocolate brownie. Let me see those toes!

You dance a waltz like this:

1,2,3, **1**,2,3

The first beat is the heaviest beat in the bar.

Left, right, right

Right, left, left

COMPOSE YOURSELF

You'll be able to find lots of famous waltzes online to listen to. One great waltz to search for is called *Scarf Dance* and was written by Cécile Chaminade, who composed during the first half of the twentieth century. She was the first female composer to be awarded the French "Légion d'Honneur," for being generally amazing. Wow, nice one, Cécile!

DOTTED NOTES

We can make notes longer by adding a dot after them. The dot adds half of the note's original value.

Dotted Note	The Same As...	Value in Beats
𝅗𝅥.	𝅗𝅥 + ♩	3
♩.	♩ + ♪	1 + 1/2

1. Everyone loves maths! Apart from Cecil. Be a buddy and mark the rest of his music homework for him.

a.) 𝅗𝅥. = 𝅗𝅥 + ♩ ✔

b.) ♩. = ♩ + ♪ ☐

c.) 𝅝 = 𝅗𝅥 + 𝅗𝅥 ☐

d.) 𝅝 = 𝅗𝅥. + ♩ ♪ ☐

e.) 𝅗𝅥. = ♩ + ♩ ☐

f.) 𝅝 = ♪ + ♪ ☐

2. Wow! Billy was out walking Dotty (his dog), when she ran through a hedge into the overgrown gardens of an old, ruined castle. And guess what? The dog furiously dug away in the grounds, revealing a shabby box containing ancient sheet music that had laid buried and undiscovered for years. Three really short pieces. But they're in such poor condition that some of the bar lines have faded away. Add them back in, making sure you've got the right number of beats in each bar.

3. Billy is playing some rhythmic studies on his drum. A study is a piece of music that helps you to practise a certain skill on your instrument or voice. Practice makes perfect, Billy!

Can you add the correct time signature at the beginning of each study?

4. Oh dear, Cecil fell asleep before he had time to add the dots to the notes in his exercises. Add the dots to complete the bars.

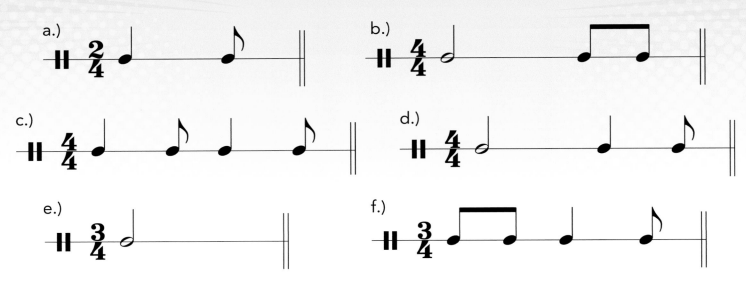

5. Billy's dog Dotty has some spots on her coat that look like musical notes. Draw an arrow to match the descriptions to the "note spots."

A dotted crotchet

A crotchet

A minim

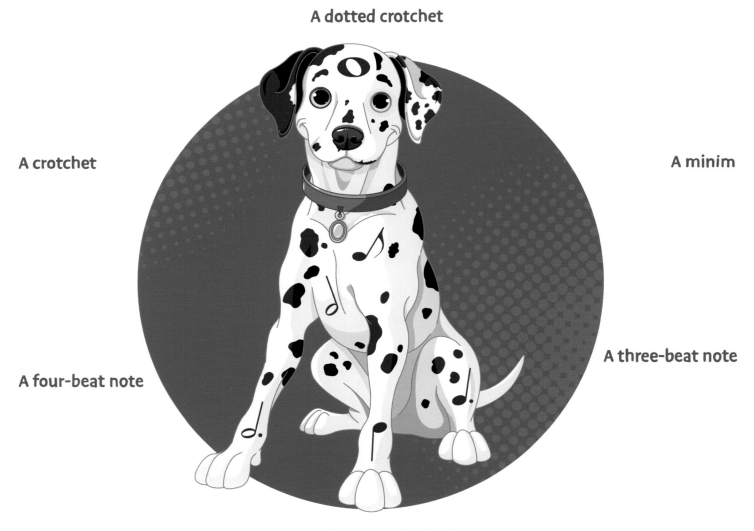

A four-beat note

A three-beat note

A note that lasts half a beat

TIES

Another way of making a note longer is to use a tie. A tie is something that smart people wear around their necks. It's also a curved line that joins together two musical notes of the same pitch. You hold through the second note instead of playing it. So, the tie "ties" the notes together!

3 beats   + 3 beats   = 6 beats

Ties are mainly used to hold notes over bar lines.

6. Join these notes with a tie and add up the sum total of crotchet beats. (There are no regular time signatures to help you, here.)

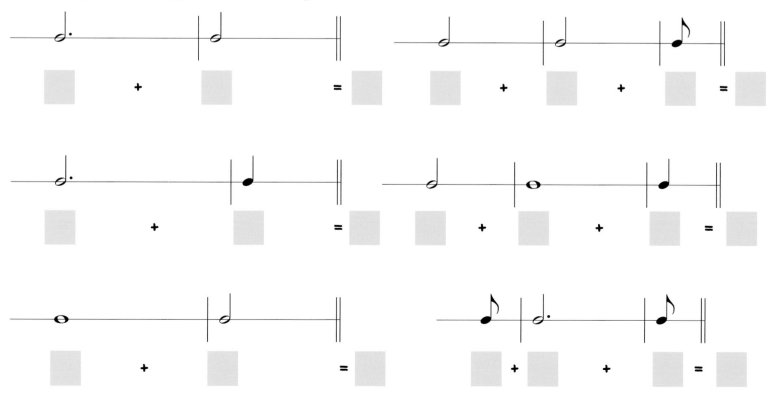

7. Look at the short piece below. Join notes of the same pitch that are next to each other with a tie. The direction of the note stem determines whether the tie curves up or down.

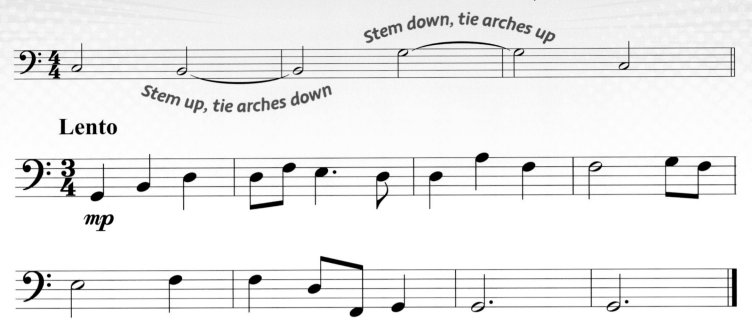

Stem down, tie arches up

Stem up, tie arches down

Lento

mp

ARTICULATION

Just as there are many ways of dancing, there are many ways of playing a note. The way that we play a note in music is called **ARTICULATION**. Take it away, Rodolpho!

LEGATO means to connect the notes smoothly, as if ice skating. Have a look at the piece below.

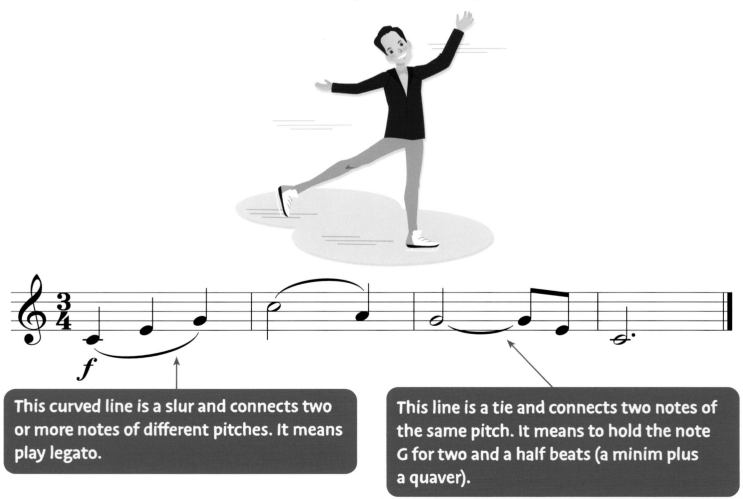

f

This curved line is a slur and connects two or more notes of different pitches. It means play legato.

This line is a tie and connects two notes of the same pitch. It means to hold the note G for two and a half beats (a minim plus a quaver).

STACCATO means to play the notes short, spiky, and detached.

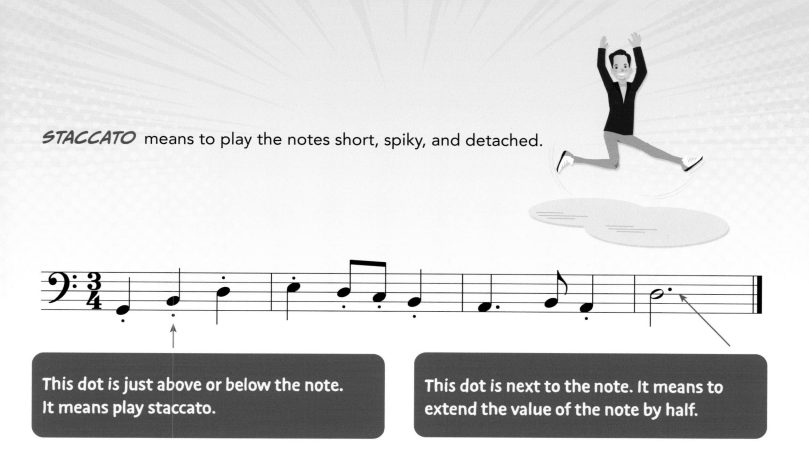

This dot is just above or below the note. It means play staccato.

This dot is next to the note. It means to extend the value of the note by half.

An *ACCENT* means to give the note a little extra force.

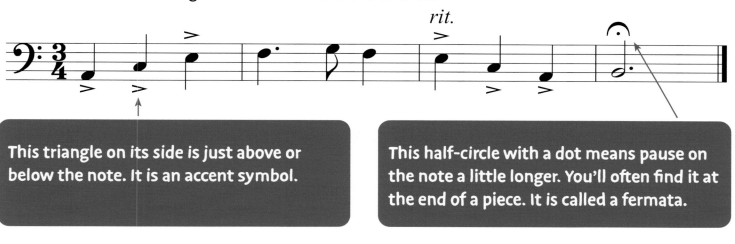

This triangle on its side is just above or below the note. It is an accent symbol.

This half-circle with a dot means pause on the note a little longer. You'll often find it at the end of a piece. It is called a fermata.

ON THE NEXT PAGE IS SOME MUSIC. IT SHOULD START STACCATO! THE THIRD AND FOURTH BARS SHOULD BE LEGATO. THE LAST TWO BARS SHOULD BE ACCENTED AND GRADUALLY SLOW DOWN. THE FINAL BAR SHOULD END WITH A PAUSE TO SHOW EVERYONE THAT THE PIECE IS FINISHED!

8. Rodolpho has just told us how he wants this piece performed, so add the missing articulation and performance markings.

WRITING MELODIES

A **MELODY** is another word for a tune. All good melodies have a strong shape and are easy to sing, like the "Happy Birthday" melody. What's your favourite melody?

MY FAVOURITE MELODY IS:_____

Some composers liked to take long walks in the countryside to help them make up melodies! They'd sometimes copy the shape of the landscape in the melody, like the example below.

CANTABILE means "in a singing style." Basically, play the melody as if you are, well, singing it. Maybe not like your dad would sing it, though.

9. Draw the shape of these two melodies in the boxes above the music.

a.)

b.)

Melodies are mostly made of steps and skips, with just the occasional bigger *LEAP*.

Step:

Skip:

Leap:

TIP FROM THE MASKED COMPOSER!

REMEMBER, THE TERMS "STEPS" AND "SKIPS" REFER TO THE GAPS BETWEEN MUSICAL NOTES.

Definition of Step:_____

Definition of Skip:_____

YOU BE THE COMPOSER!

GASP. Another text from Rodolpho!

Quick, it's almost opening night at the ballet! How's that melody coming?

I want the waltz to be smooth to begin with and then have lots of short, spiky notes. It should finish with a fermata at the end. Oh, and use lots of lovely dynamics! It's going to bring the house down (not literally)!

SAY WHAT?!

In Switzerland, it is illegal to mow the lawn while dressed as Elvis Presley.

DAD JOKE CORNER

WHAT MAKES MUSIC ON YOUR HEAD?

A HEADBAND!

10. It's your turn. Compose eight bars of music for Rodolpho's ballet on ice. He's given you the starting note and the finishing note.

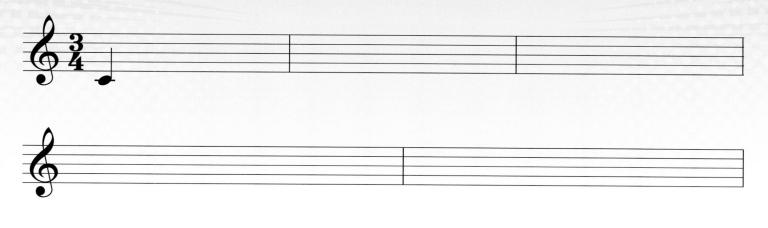

TIP FROM THE MASKED COMPOSER!

MAKE SURE YOUR MELODY HAS A STRONG SHAPE. YOU MIGHT WANT TO LIGHTLY DRAW THE SHAPE OUT FIRST ON THE STAVE BEFORE PUTTING IN THE NOTES! AND REMEMBER TO CHECK RODOLPHO'S TEXT SO YOU GIVE HIM WHAT HE WANTS!

COMPOSE YOURSELF

The Russian composer Pyotr Il'yich Tchaikovsky composed some of the most famous ballet music ever written. Much of it is still played today and features in lots of films. You know the song "Once Upon a Dream" from the classic Disney production *Sleeping Beauty*? Well, the music is actually a waltz by Tchaikovsky! (Oh, and he only went and wrote a piece of music with actual cannons firing in it. CANNONS?! Don't believe it? Just search for the *1812 Overture* and have a listen. It'll blow you away!)

HOW DO I FEEL?

We learnt all about the $\frac{3}{4}$ *TIME SIGNATURE* and the *WALTZ, DOTTED NOTES, TIES, ARTICULATION*, and how to shape a *MELODY*. How do you think you did with this chapter?

Yes, I understand all of this.	🙂	Can you play your waltz on your instrument? If not, ask someone to play it for you!
I think I understand but some bits were tricky.	😐	Great job for realising this. Look through the notes again and ask your teacher about the tricky bits.
I still don't understand most of it.	🙁	Hey, all of us struggle sometimes. Go over from the beginning with your teacher or another adult. To get some extra help, download more worksheet exercises, here. 

MY THEORY SCRAPBOOK

$\frac{3}{4}$: "Three-four" time. The time signature that shows us we have three crotchet beats in a bar.

Waltz: A type of dance that has three beats per bar.

Dotted Note: A note that has its value extended by half, by virtue of a dot next to the notehead.

Dotted Minim ♩.: A note value worth three beats.

Dotted Crotchet ♩.: A note value worth one and a half beats (a crotchet plus a quaver).

Tie: A curved line connecting two notes of the same pitch, indicating they are to be played as one note.

Articulation: Word to describe how musical notes are to be played (like smooth or spiky).

Legato: Italian articulation word, directing the performer to play notes in a smooth manner. (Shown by a curved line called a slur connecting different pitches.)

Staccato: Italian articulation word, directing the performer to play notes in a spiky, detached manner. (Shown by a dot above or below the notehead.)

$>$: Accent symbol. Directs the performer to play a note with extra force.

⌒: Fermata symbol. Directs the performer to hold onto a note for longer than its value.

Melody: The part of music that you sing or hum along to. A memorable collection of notes, also known as a "tune."

Hoodini: An owl magician.

CHAPTER 5
THE FUNKY DRUMMER

> ### MUSICAL TOPICS
> Semiquavers, rests, dotted quaver, the drum kit, repeat marks, and beaming.

Billy has got a new instrument for his birthday. It's a brand-new drum kit! He is super excited. His neighbour Alfonzo is less thrilled about it.

Hey Billy! *POCO* less *FORTISSIMO*. I'm trying to sleep here! You need to *DIMINUENDO* and learn to play *PIANISSIMO*. And you're *ACCELERANDO*: typical drummer!

1. Translate what Alfonzo is saying below.

Hey Billy! _____ less _____. I'm trying to sleep here!

You need to _____ and learn to play _____.

And you're _____: typical drummer!

Mmm… maybe Billy needs to practise a little more. Luckily, there's a fantastic composer in the neighbourhood to help him out. Who's that, you say? It's—drum roll—YOU!

Billy's neighbour Alfonzo will be impressed! At least we hope so, or it's no more pizza for Billy.

SEMIQUAVERS

Semiquavers are worth 1/4 of a beat. (There are four semiquavers in one crotchet. There are two semiquavers in one quaver.)

A single quaver has one flag but a single semiquaver has two flags:

When there are four in a row, they can all hold hands and be grouped together, like this.

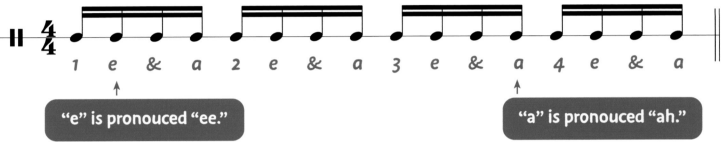

Four semiquavers make four sounds to one beat. You can count semiquavers like this.

Here's a rhythm tree, showing how the note values we've learnt so far fit together.

2. Write these note values out in the box below, ordered from shortest to longest.

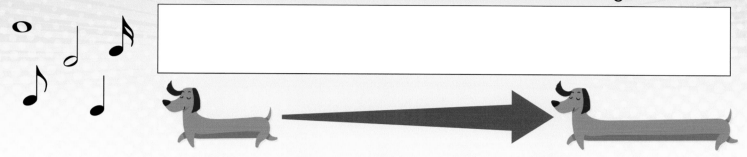

3. Do some sums with the note values, making the answer one note only!

a.) ♪ + ♪ =

b.) ♫ =

c.) ♬ =

d.) ♩ + ♩ =

e.) ♪ + ♪ + ♪ =

f.) ♩ + ♩ =

g.) ♫ + ♬ + ♩ =

h.) ♫ + ♬ =

4. Billy has been practising while eating Alfonzo's delicious pizza. Write one note value on each pizza-sauce splodge to make the bars complete.

Remember, this clef is called the percussion clef.

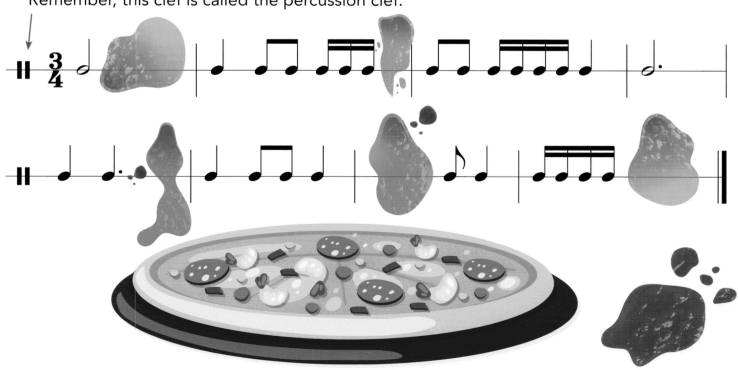

5. Hayley is practising a tricky piece with lots of different rhythms. Let's help her figure it out. Draw a line to connect the descriptions to the notes. The first one has been done for you.

The note "G" as a minim

Any note worth 1/4 of a beat

Any note with a fermata

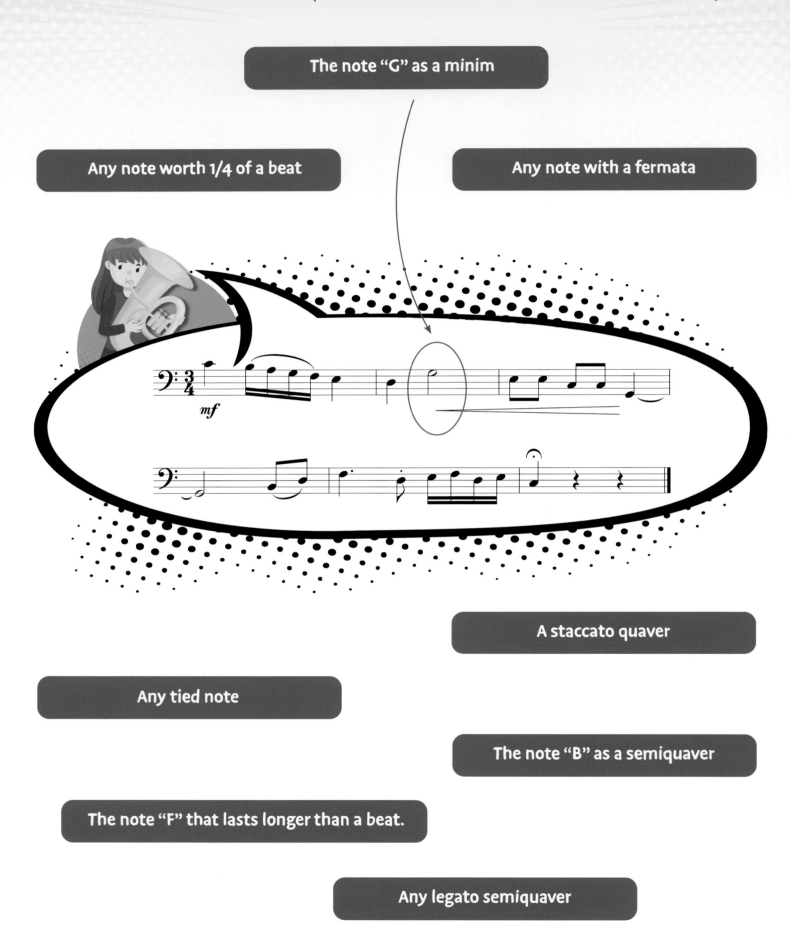

A staccato quaver

Any tied note

The note "B" as a semiquaver

The note "F" that lasts longer than a beat.

Any legato semiquaver

RESTS

A rest indicates a moment of silence. Silence is very important. Have you ever been kept awake by annoying loud noises at night? Then, you'll understand!

Here are some different kinds of rests.

Name	Rest	Value	Description
Semibreve Rest	▬	4 beats **or** the whole bar	A rectangular blob hanging below the second-highest stave line. (Below the line because it's "heavy.")
Minim Rest	▬	2 beats	A rectangular blob sitting on top of the middle stave line. (On top of the line because it's "lighter" than the semibreve rest.)
Crotchet Rest	𝄽	1 beat	A squished-up "3" with a curl on the bottom.
Quaver Rest	𝄾	1/2 beat	A fancy-pants number "7."
Semiquaver Rest	𝄿	1/4 beat	A fancy-pants number "7" with an extra flag.

The rectangular blob hanging below the second-highest line means a four-beat rest. But it can also mean silence for the entire bar. It doesn't matter what time signature you're in, it will always mean a whole bar of silence.

SHHHHHHHHHHHHHHHHHHHHHHHHHHHHHHHHHHHHHHHHHHHHHHHHH

6. Rests can be tricky to draw but, as we know, practice makes perfect!

   Practise drawing the rests out on the staves below. Under each rest, write its beat value.

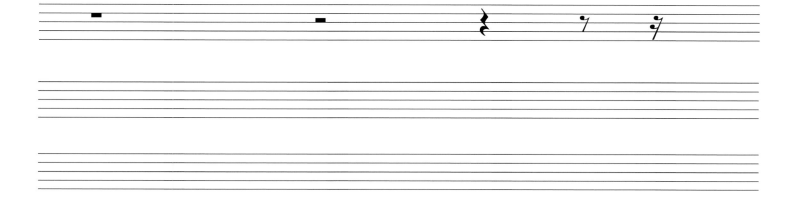

7. Work out how many beats are in these bars and add the time signature.

8. One of the notes on Hayley's tuba has stopped working. Write out the music again but use a rest every time she gets to the starred notes.

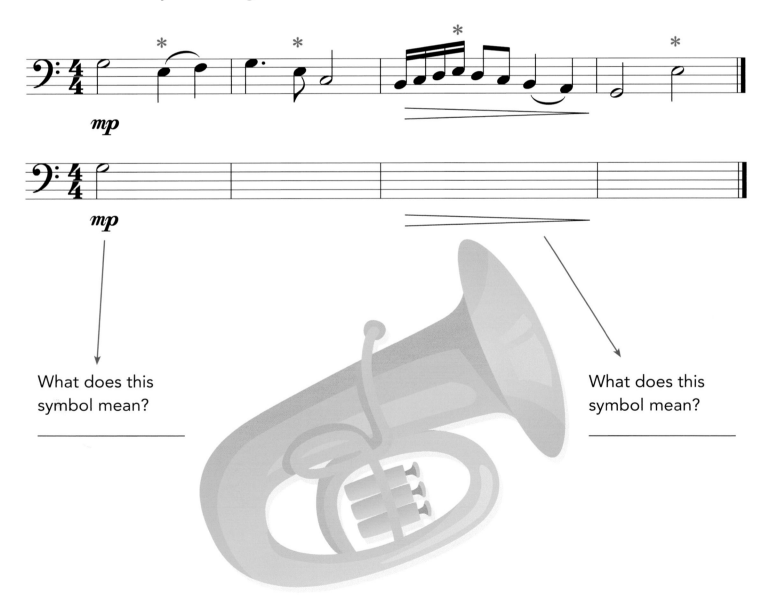

What does this symbol mean?

_____

What does this symbol mean?

_____

What is the note that Hayley's tuba couldn't play? _____

THE DRUM KIT

Let's take a closer look at Billy's new birthday present. The drum kit is actually a collection of instruments from all over the world.

The **CYMBALS** were invented in Asia in ancient times. They were even used by the Romans! They are made by hammering sheets of bronze metal.

The **HI-HAT** was invented in America at the beginning of the 20th century. The two cymbals can be played with a foot pedal.

The **TOM-TOMS** are tuned to different pitches. They are versions of west African drums like the djembe.

People have been using the **SNARE** drum since medieval times. It has wires on the back to make it sound extra rattily!

The **BASS DRUM** is the same sort of instrument played in marching bands. When it's played as part of a drum kit, the drummer uses a foot pedal.

One drummer on a drum kit can do the work of several percussion players!

TIP FROM THE MASKED COMPOSER!

THE NEXT FEW EXERCISES WILL INVOLVE THE TERM "OSTINATO." WE'VE USED THIS BEFORE BUT IF YOU NEED A REMINDER OF ITS MEANING, GO BACK TO YOUR "SCRAP BOOK" AT THE END OF CHAPTER 1.

9. a.) The bass drum likes to play on the first and third beats of each bar.
Write out the ostinato for two more bars. The final rest has been written for you.

1 (2) 3 &(4)   1 (2) 3 &(4)   1 (2) 3 & (4)   1 (2) 3 & (4)

b.) The snare drum usually plays on the second and fourth beats of each bar.
Write out the ostinato for two more bars.

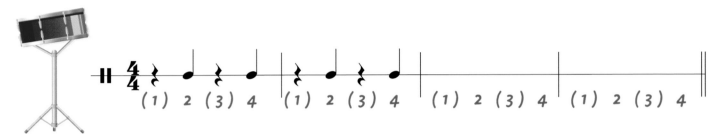

(1) 2 (3) 4   (1) 2 (3) 4   (1) 2 (3) 4   (1) 2 (3) 4

c.) The hi-hat usually plays short-value notes like quavers or semiquavers all the way
through the bar. Write out the ostinato for two more bars.

1 & 2 & 3 & 4 &   1 & 2 & 3 & 4 &

1 & 2 & 3 & 4 &   1 & 2 & 3 & 4 &

This is how they all fit together.

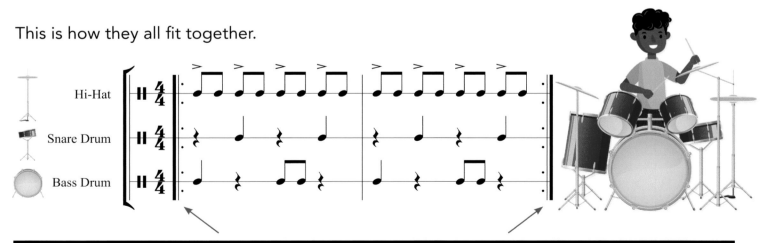

Hi-Hat

Snare Drum

Bass Drum

This double bar line with dots is called a repeat mark or repeat bar line.
The music that lies in between two sets of these is to be repeated.

GROUPING NOTES TOGETHER

Short-value notes like to hang out together in groups of one beat. They're joined by one or more lines across the top called a **BEAM**. We've already come across this when we looked at quavers and semiquavers holding hands.

You can see that this music looks a bit messy and confusing.

When beamed into single-beat groups, this is now much easier for a musician to read.

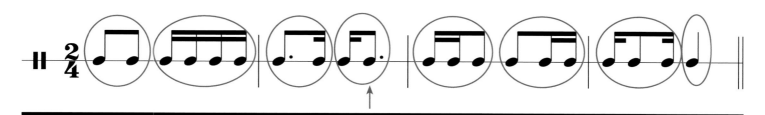

This is a dotted quaver. It's worth 3/4 of a beat. There are three semiquavers in one dotted quaver.

You'll mostly see a dotted quaver joined to a semiquaver by a beam. This makes a single, crotchet beat.

10. Write out these bars again so that the notes are beamed together in groups of one beat.

Occasionally, Cecil gets a bit confused between playing his dotted crotchets and his dotted quavers. And that's fair enough, all those dots can drive you a bit dotty! One day, he receives a secret envelope in the mail.

Inside is a useful cheat sheet, showing how these dotted notes count differently. And it's been signed *from the Masked Composer*. Who on earth is this musical hero?

You can practise using the Masked Composer's cheat sheet by clapping the rhythm and counting the beat count. Remember to keep the beat steady.

1 (e&) a   2 (e&) a   3 (e&) a   4 (e&) a   1   (& 2) &   3   (& 4) &

DAD JOKE CORNER

WHAT TYPES OF SONGS DO PLANETS SING?

NEP-TUNES!

YOU BE THE COMPOSER!

11. It's your turn to write a brand-new drum rhythm for Billy to practise. Something so funky that not even Alfonzo will complain!

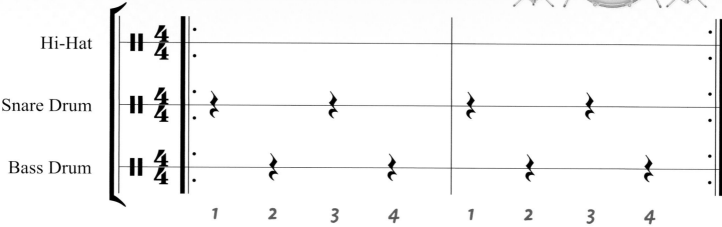

> **Above, compose a hi-hat rhythm that uses quavers and semiquavers. Make sure you beam the notes correctly.**

> **Above, compose a snare drum rhythm that lasts one beat. You should use a mixture of crotchets and quavers. Put it on the second and fourth beats of each bar.**

> **Above, compose a bass drum rhythm that lasts one beat. You should use a mixture of crotchets and quavers. Put it on the first and third beats of each bar.**

Why not get two other people to perform your drum rhythm with you?

COMPOSE YOURSELF

One of the most famous ostinatos ever was written by the French composer Maurice Ravel in his piece *Boléro* from the 1920s. It became super popular and was even used in a gold-medal winning ice-skating routine. Ravel actually said he didn't like the piece. But we love it anyway, Maurice! Go on, have a listen!

HOW DO I FEEL?

In this chapter, we learnt about *SEMIQUAVERS*, *RESTS*, *THE DRUM KIT*, *DOTTED QUAVERS*, and how to *BEAM* notes together. How did you do with this chapter?

Yes, I understand all of this.	🙂	Try writing some more drum rhythms with dotted note values and performing them with friends.
I think I understand but some bits were tricky.	😐	Great job for realising this. Look through the notes again and ask your teacher about the tricky bits.
I still don't understand most of it.	🙁	Hey, all of us struggle sometimes. Go over from the beginning with your teacher or another adult. To get some extra help, download more worksheet exercises, here. 

MY THEORY SCRAPBOOK

Semiquaver ♬: A note value worth 1/4 of a beat. There are four semiquavers in a crotchet beat (♬♬).

𝄥 : The percussion-clef symbol, used for unpitched percussion instruments.

▬ : A semibreve-rest symbol, indicating four beats of silence. It also signifies a whole bar of silence.

▬ : A minim-rest symbol, indicating two beats of silence.

𝄽 : A crotchet-rest symbol, indicating one beat of silence.

Beam: To join quavers and semiquavers together into single-beat units with one or two horizontal lines.

𝄾 : A quaver-rest symbol, indicating half a beat of silence.

𝄿 : A semiquaver-rest symbol, indicating 1/4 of a beat's worth of silence.

𝄇 : A repeat mark. Music that lies in between two sets of these bar lines with dots is to be repeated.

Drum Kit: A set of drums and cymbals organised so that one person can play them.

Dotted Quaver ♪.: A note value worth 3/4 of a beat (a quaver plus a semiquaver).

Satisfactory: Where average things are manufactured.

CHAPTER 6
THE MONSTER SHOW

It's Adagietta Maestra, again!

DARLING! YOU DID SUCH GREAT WORK ON THE SPY FILM. EVERYONE LOVED IT! SO, EXCITING NEWS. I HAVE A NEW TV SHOW. IT'S ALL ABOUT MONSTERS AND I NEED A CREEPY MELODY FOR THE THEME TUNE. I KNOW YOU'LL BE JUST PERFECT. GOT TO GO. CIAO, DARLING! XXX

Another commission! At this rate, you're going to be the busiest composer in town.

Before we write the theme tune, we need to learn some new bits of music theory to make our melody extra scary and extra catchy.

In this chapter, you may want to refer back to your treble and bass notes. If so, use the grand staff on page 108. This work is going to be a challenge but don't worry…

YOU'VE GOT THIS.

SEMITONES

A *SEMITONE* is the smallest gap between two notes. This is what semitones look like on the piano keyboard.

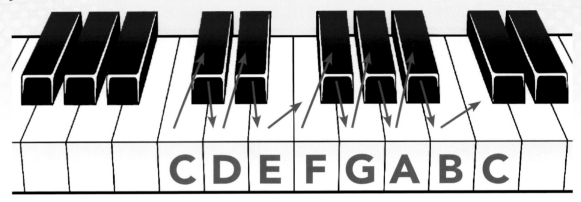

Mostly, it's simple to see semitones on a piano keyboard. This is because a semitone is usually between a black key and a white key.

But not always.

1. Can you spot two places where a semitone is between two white keys?

Between note ___ and note ___

AND

Between note ___ and note ___

2. Play a semitone on your instrument. (Or you could sing a semitone.) The notes are so close that you can almost hear them rubbing against each other!

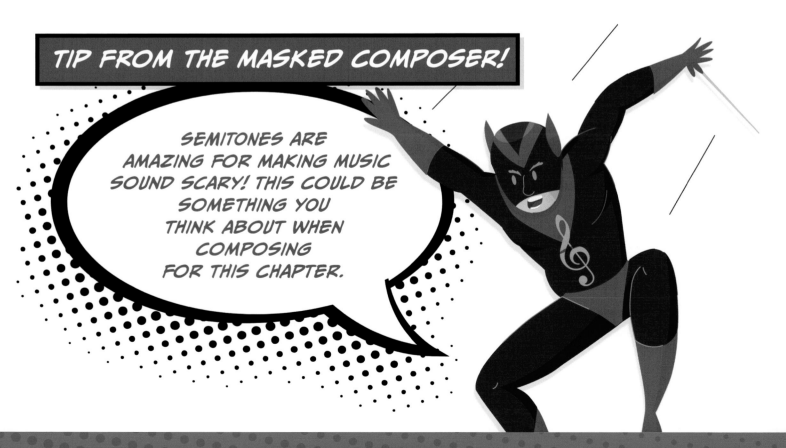

TIP FROM THE MASKED COMPOSER!

SEMITONES ARE AMAZING FOR MAKING MUSIC SOUND SCARY! THIS COULD BE SOMETHING YOU THINK ABOUT WHEN COMPOSING FOR THIS CHAPTER.

SHARPS AND FLATS

♯ A *SHARP* sign raises a note by a semitone. It looks a bit like a hashtag.

♭ A *FLAT* sign lowers a note by a semitone. It looks a bit like a squashed-up letter "b."

♮ A *NATURAL* sign is a way of saying a "normal" note. It is used to cancel out a previous sharp or flat. It looks like a diamond with two lines sticking out of it.

Together, sharps, flats, and naturals are known as *ACCIDENTALS*.

3. Practise drawing accidentals by decorating the **DREADED ACCIDENTAL MONSTER!**

DECORATE HIS LEGS WITH NATURAL SIGNS.

DECORATE HIS CHEEKS WITH FLAT SIGNS.

DECORATE HIS NOSE WITH SHARP SIGNS.

Accidentals always come **before** the note. This is so the musician can prepare the note in advance. Imagine only realising your F was actually an F-sharp after you had played it!

They need to be carefully written in a space or on a line.

4. Add an accidental to change the note and write the note name underneath.

a.) Make this C a C-sharp by adding a sharp sign before the notehead.

b.) Make this F an F-sharp by adding a sharp sign before the notehead.

c.) Make this G a G-flat by adding a flat sign before the notehead.

d.) Make this E an E-flat by adding a flat sign before the notehead.

5. In this part of Adagietta's TV show, the monster is creeping up and down the stairs.

a.) First, let's write the music for when the monster is creeping up the stairs. Look at the stave below. Use an accidental on each starred note to make it a semitone higher. The first one has been done for you.

b.) Now, let's write the music for when the monster is creeping down the stairs. Look at the stave below. Use an accidental on each starred note to make it a semitone lower. The first one has been done for you.

6. Let's compose a study for Cecil so he can practise his semitones. Using only crotchets, write the pitches that are indicated above the stave. Each note should be a semitone from the one before.

You might already have noticed that each black key on the piano keyboard actually has two different names. Here's an example:

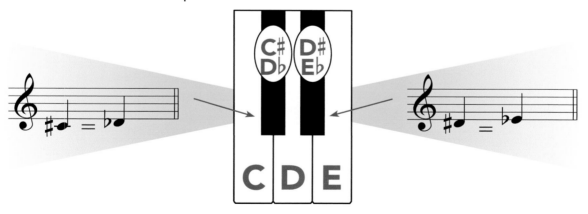

The notes C♯ and D♭ sound the same and share the same key on the piano keyboard. So, we have two different names for the same pitch.

The notes D♯ and E♭ sound the same and share the same key on the piano keyboard. So, we have two different names for the same pitch.

7. Draw a line connecting the notes that look different but sound exactly the same. One has been done for you.

TONES

A *TONE* is made up of two semitones. Here, you can see an example of some tones on a piano keyboard.

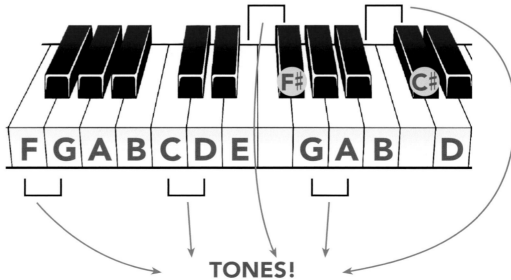

8. In another part of Adagietta's TV show, a monster is in a hurry and is running up the stairs, taking the steps two at a time. Write music that shows this. In the empty ovals on the stave below, write the note that's a tone higher or lower than the note before it. Copy the articulation markings and watch out, you might have to use accidentals!

a.) In each green oval, write the note that's a tone higher than the note before it.

b.) In each blue oval, write the note that's a tone lower than the note before it.

9. It's time to play everyone's favourite Saturday-night game show…

Write "T" for tone and "S" for semitone. Remember, there are fabulous prizes to be won!*

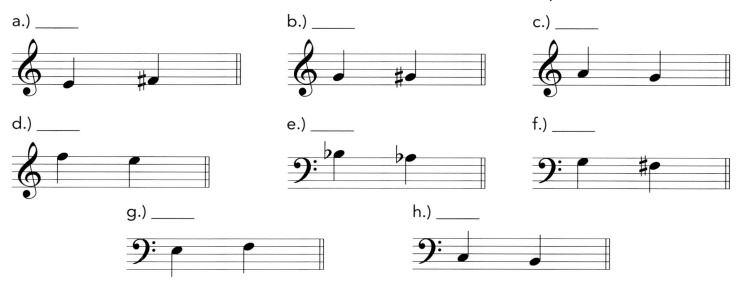

a.) _____   b.) _____   c.) _____

d.) _____   e.) _____   f.) _____

g.) _____   h.) _____

There aren't actually any prizes. We've run out. Sorry about that.

NATURALS

A natural sign cancels out a sharp or flat that comes before it.

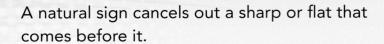

The natural sign turns this note back into a "normal B" note.

DON'T BE SHARP. DON'T BE FLAT. JUST BE NATURAL!

Accidentals last for not just the note but the whole bar! Back in the day, composers liked to save ink and didn't want to write out the accidental every time it happened. No, seriously, ink was expensive stuff in the past. Still is.

WHOOPS!

This note is still an F-sharp (F#). But the accidental doesn't carry over the bar line.

This note is now an F-natural (F♮) because it's in a new bar.

Sometimes, composers will help you remember this by putting the natural accidental in brackets. (But only if they're in a good mood!)

10. Add a natural sign before the starred notes to cancel the accidentals.

a.)

b.)

c.)

d.)

11. Let's now compose a semitone study for Hayley. Using only crotchets, write the pitches that are indicated above the stave. Each note should be a semitone from the one before.

C   C#   D   D#   E   F   F♮   E   Eb   D   Db   C   B

When a note is tied over the bar line, the accidental lasts for the whole duration.

THE OTHER DAY, I WROTE A SONG ABOUT A TORTILLA.

WELL, ACTUALLY IT WAS MORE OF A WRAP!

DAD JOKE CORNER

YOU BE THE COMPOSER!

12. It's time to write that theme tune to Adagietta's Monster TV show. Let's follow the action on the screen.

THE MONSTER CREEPS DOWN THE STAIRS.

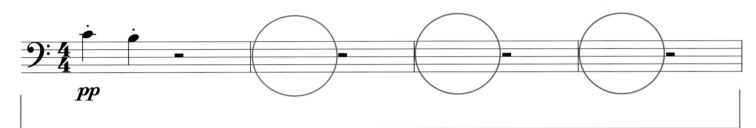

Here, use pairs of crotchet notes a semitone apart going down. Write them in the ovals on the stave.

THEN, IT STOMPS ALONG THE HALLWAY.

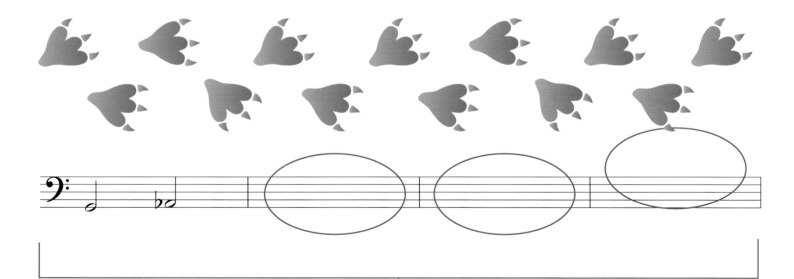

Here, use pairs of minims a semitone apart going up.

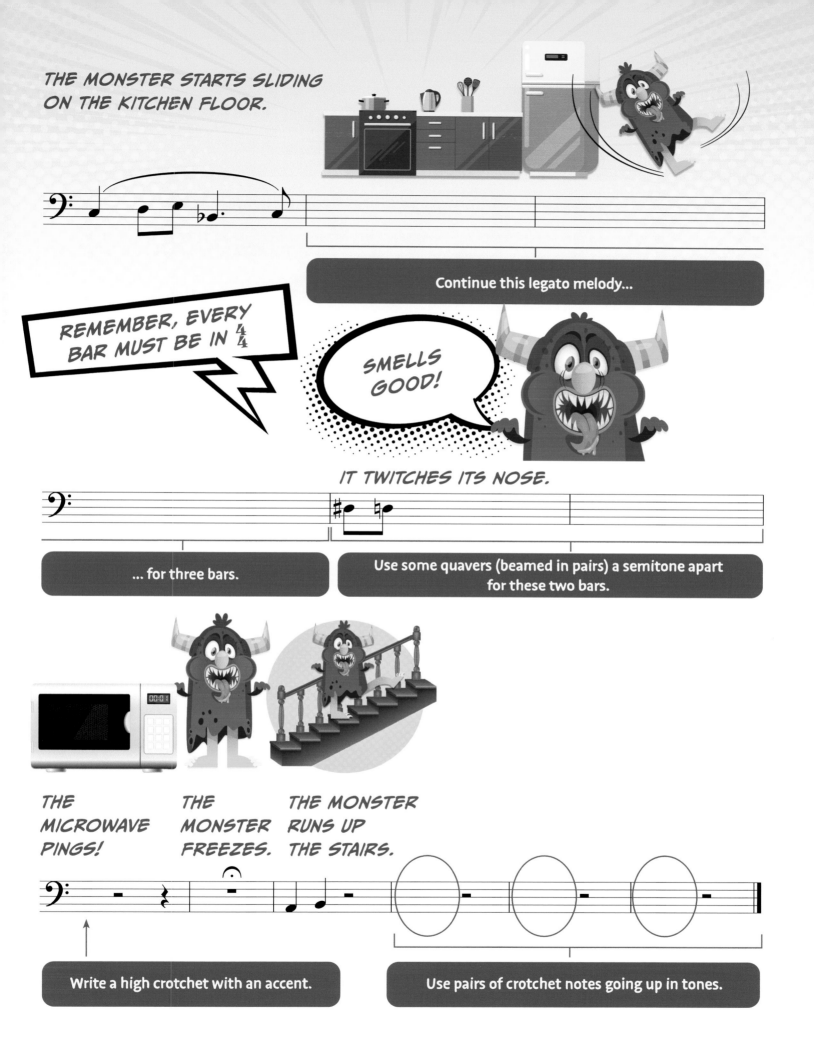

THE MONSTER STARTS SLIDING ON THE KITCHEN FLOOR.

Continue this legato melody...

REMEMBER, EVERY BAR MUST BE IN $\frac{4}{4}$

SMELLS GOOD!

IT TWITCHES ITS NOSE.

... for three bars.

Use some quavers (beamed in pairs) a semitone apart for these two bars.

THE MICROWAVE PINGS!

THE MONSTER FREEZES.

THE MONSTER RUNS UP THE STAIRS.

Write a high crotchet with an accent.

Use pairs of crotchet notes going up in tones.

COMPOSE YOURSELF

Ever heard of John Williams? Williams is probably the most famous film composer of all time. *E.T.*, *Jurassic Park*, *Home Alone*, *Star Wars*, *Superman*, *Harry Potter*: you've guessed it, music by John Williams! He also wrote music to a film called *Jaws*, which was all about a huge, scary shark. He used lots of semitones and accidentals in his music to show just how frightening it would be if a shark surprised you while you were swimming.

HOW DO I FEEL?

We've learnt all about **SHARPS**, **FLATS**, **NATURALS**, **TONES**, and **SEMITONES**.
How did you do with this chapter?

Yes, I understand all of this.	🙂	Try writing another monster composition where the music shows something different happening.
I think I understand but some bits were tricky.	😐	Great job for realising this. Look through the notes again and ask your teacher about the tricky bits.
I still don't understand most of it.	🙁	Hey, all of us struggle sometimes. Go over from the beginning with your teacher or another adult. To get some extra help, download more worksheet exercises, here. Download

MY THEORY SCRAPBOOK

Semitone: The smallest gap between two notes.

Tone: A gap between two notes that consists of two semitones.

Sharp: A musical symbol showing a note has been raised by a semitone. Sharpened notes are depicted by the ♯ symbol before the notehead on the stave.

Flat: A musical symbol showing a note has been lowered by a semitone. Flattened notes are depicted by the ♭ symbol before the notehead on the stave.

Natural: A musical symbol showing a note should return to its original pitch, cancelling out sharp or flat notes. This is depicted by the ♮ symbol before the notehead on the stave.

Accidental: The collective name for sharp, flat, and natural symbols.

Infantry: An army of babies.

CHAPTER 7
FISHY SCALES

MUSICAL TOPICS

Scales patterns and key signatures (C major, G major, D major, F major).

Cecil has a performance exam coming up and he's pretty nervous about playing his scales.

… no, not that kind of scale.

… nor that kind of scale.

A musical *SCALE* is a collection of notes that move by step. You might well have already played some on an instrument.

They're great for loads of reasons. Scales are like going to the gym for musicians. They build our muscle strength and train our brains!

But there's another reason for learning about scales. They are the building blocks of many styles of music. If you know about scales, you'll understand how a lot of music is built.

We're going to help Cecil by writing him a piece with lots of scales. He'll be practising scales without even knowing. Genius!

We'll need to know about scale "DNA" and *KEY SIGNATURES*. Don't worry, Cecil, we've got your back!

SCALE DNA

In science, DNA is the code that controls the way our bodies are built.

Scales also have a DNA code, made up of a mixture of tones and semitones.

Here's a scale starting on the note C. It's called the scale of **C MAJOR**. It's **ASCENDING** (going up, getting higher in pitch). On a piano, the C major scale uses only white keys; there are no sharps or flats.

T = Tone   **S** = Semitone

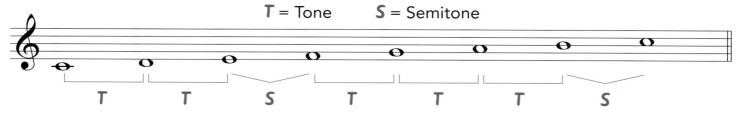

1. a.) Write out the C major scale ascending and **DESCENDING** (going down, getting lower in pitch).

    b.) Write in the musical DNA code for the descending half of the scale in tones and semitones.

TIP FROM THE MASKED COMPOSER!

IT WILL REALLY HELP IF YOU TRY AND MEMORISE THE PATTERN OF TONES AND SEMITONES FOR A MAJOR SCALE, BOTH FOR CHECKING YOUR WORK AND PLAYING SCALES ON YOUR INSTRUMENT!

2. a.) Write out the scale of C major ascending and descending in the bass clef for Hayley to play. Use semibreves only.

   b.) Draw a bracket ⌐____⌐ below the tones.

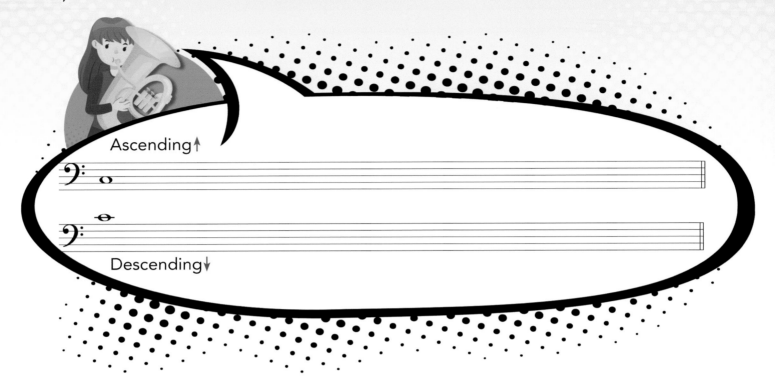

WRITING MAJOR SCALES

It doesn't matter what note we start on, the DNA code of the major scale always stays the same.

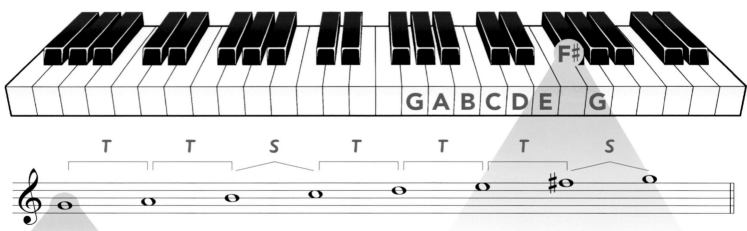

A scale gets its name from the note it starts on. This is a G major scale.

Notice that the scale of G major contains an accidental: F♯

3. Write the G major scale in the bass clef. Use semibreves and don't forget the accidental! Then, write the pattern of tones and semitones underneath.

4. Circle the semitone intervals in this tune. The first one has been done for you.

KEY SIGNATURES

As we know, ink was very expensive and some composers could be kind of lazy. For example, if they were composing a piece based on the G major scale, they didn't want to write in a # sign by every single "F" note.

So, in the end they stuck the accidentals at the beginning of the music on the stave. They called this a *KEY SIGNATURE*. It tells the musician what notes will always have a particular accidental in front of them. It's then up to the performer to remember. A bit unfair but then, that's composers for you.

URGH, WRITING ACCIDENTALS IS SOOOO DULL. THAT'S WHY I LOVE C MAJOR. THE KEY SIGNATURE HAS NOTHING IN IT! AH, C MAJOR. GOOD TIMES.

Look at the music again for Question 4. It would be so much easier for the composer to write in one, universal F-sharp sign at the beginning of the music than have to mark every "F" note with a #.

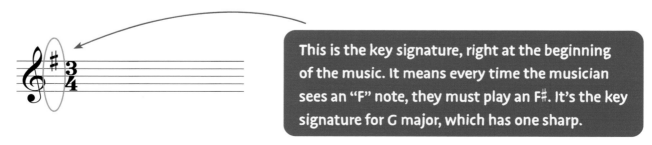

This is the key signature, right at the beginning of the music. It means every time the musician sees an "F" note, they must play an F#. It's the key signature for G major, which has one sharp.

G MAJOR

5. These are the key signatures of G major. Copy them out as many times as you like on the blank staves provided. Copy the time signature too, so you get used to writing the correct symbol order.

6. Here's one of the pieces that Cecil has been learning for his exam. All those sharp signs are confusing! Add a key signature in the oval and write it out again on the blank stave without the accidentals.

The key signature always comes before the time signature.

D MAJOR

7. The scale of D major has two sharps. The names of these sharps are _____ and _____.

8. Draw a line from each fish to the correct fish tank. You can check if your tones and semitones are in the right order by referring back to your work on the C major and G major scales.

9. These are the key signatures of D major. Copy them out in the empty staves below.

10. Trick Cecil into practising his scale by making it into a fun melody! Write out the D major scale in the rhythm given above the stave.

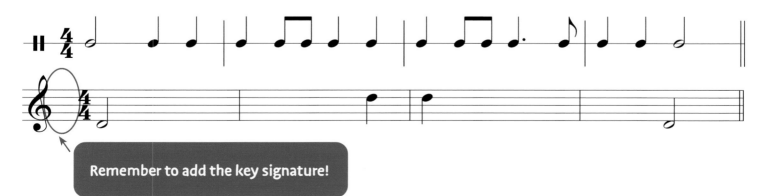

Remember to add the key signature!

F MAJOR

11. The scale of F major doesn't use sharps at all. It has one flat. The name of the flat is _____.

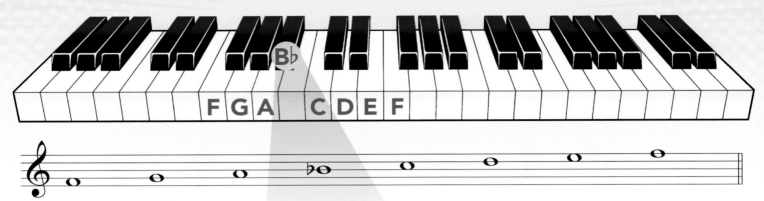

12. These are the key signatures of F major. Copy them out in the empty staves below.

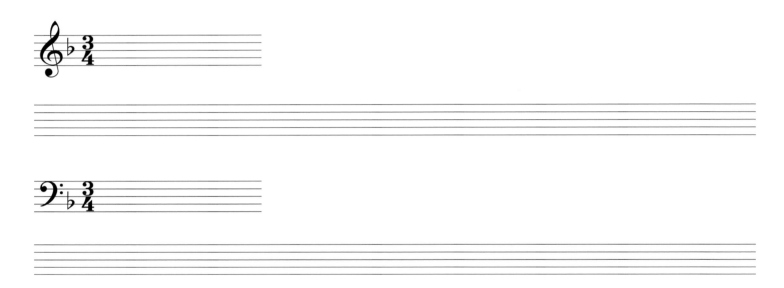

13. Write out the complete scale of F major in the bass clef for Hayley to play. The first and last notes have been written for you. Use crotchets and, instead of writing the key signature, write in every necessary accidental.

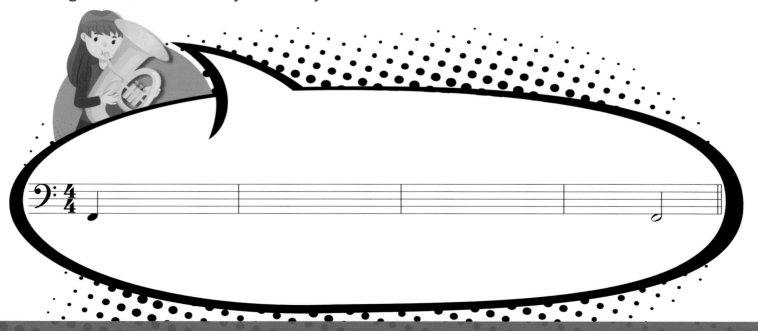

14. Here are some key signatures, written inside some scaly fish! Identify each major key signature, writing the answer in the space below the fish. One has been done for you.

C major

_____   _____

_____   _____   _____

KEY COLOUR

Some composers think that each key has its own special feeling or colour. Here's what was written in a theory book (sort of like this one) over 300 years ago. Do you agree? Have someone play the scales you've learnt and colour in the key-signature fish using the colour you believe best fits the feeling of the key.

C Major	Joyful and war-like
G Major	Serious and magnificent
D Major	Joyous and very war-like
F Major	Furious and quick-tempered

From Charpentier's *Règles de Composition*, 1682

WHAT'S THE DIFFERENCE BETWEEN A FISH AND A PIANO?

DAD JOKE CORNER

YOU CAN'T TUNA FISH!

YOU BE THE COMPOSER!

15. Let's write a trick piece for Cecil or Hayley (a piece that is secretly just a scale).

    a.) Choose a clef and write it at the beginning of the stave.

    b.) Choose a scale and write its key signature next to the clef.

    c.) Choose a time signature: $\frac{2}{4}$, $\frac{3}{4}$, or $\frac{4}{4}$.

    d.) Write out the scale in any rhythm you like, ascending and descending, as long as it correctly fills the four bars on the stave.

    e.) Add lots of dynamics, articulation, and musical expressions. Turn it into a piece!

    f.) Write a final bar line at the end.

    g.) Remember to begin and end on the note that the scale is named after. (If it's a C major scale, begin and end on the note "C.")

HOW DO I FEEL?

In this chapter, we've learnt about *SCALE DNA*, *FOUR MAJOR KEYS*, and *KEY SIGNATURES*!

Yes, I understand all of this.	☺	Try writing another "scales piece." Use a different scale and clef from your last one.
I think I understand but some bits were tricky.	😐	Great job for realising this. Look through the notes again and ask your teacher about the tricky bits.
I still don't understand most of it.	☹	Hey, all of us struggle sometimes. Go over from the beginning with your teacher or another adult. To get some extra help, download more worksheet exercises, here. 

MY THEORY SCRAPBOOK

Scale: A stepwise progression of notes in a specific order.

Major Scale: A scale that has a set pattern of tones and semitones. (T–T–S–T–T–T–S.)

Key Signature: The sharps or flats written on the stave at the beginning of a piece to indicate the key.

C Major: A key that contains no sharps or flats.

G Major: A key that contains one sharp (F♯).

D Major: A key that contains two sharps (F♯ and C♯).

F Major: A key that contains one flat (B♭).

Ascending: Musical notes going up (getting higher in pitch).

Descending: Musical notes going down (getting lower in pitch).

Popcorn: A snack with a hit song.

CHAPTER 8
FANFARE FOR THE MAYOR

MUSICAL TOPICS
Degrees of the scale, triads, and intervals.

Mr Crotchety has exciting news!

> ATTENTION, PUPILS! THAT MEANS YOU, CECIL.
>
> THE MAYOR IS OPENING THE LOCAL SWIMMING CENTRE AND THE SCHOOL ORCHESTRA HAS BEEN INVITED TO PLAY!

> INAPPROPRIATE TIME TO ASK FOR A WALK?

The orchestra will have to play just the right piece of music. Something bold, brassy, and brilliant. A fanfare!

Disaster! Dotty has eaten all of the orchestral parts. Looks like the opening of the swimming centre will have to be cancelled. If only there were a composer who could write something for the orchestra! Oh well, the whole town will just have to be disappointed and the day will be completely ruined forever.

Hang on! YOU are a composer!

So, let's get to it. The whole town wants a swim!

To write an amazing fanfare for the orchestra, we will need to learn about degrees of the scale, tonic triads, and intervals.

DEGREES OF THE SCALE

Each note of the scale has its own number, depending on where it appears in the scale order. In music theory, rather than saying "scale number," we say *DEGREE*.

"K" is for keynote. The keynote is the most important degree of the scale. Pieces often begin and end on the keynote.

1. Mr Crotchety is shouting out notes to play. Write the note name of the degrees of the scale in C major.

   a.) Fifth degree! _____   b.) Keynote! _____   c.) Seventh degree! _____

   d.) Second degree! _____   e.) Third degree! _____   f.) Fourth degree! _____

2. Fill in the notes of the other scales. Remember to write in the accidentals.

| Keynote | Second degree | Third degree | Fourth degree | Fifth degree | Sixth degree | Seventh degree | Keynote |

G Major

D Major

F Major

3. The orchestra is getting ready for the big day with some note drills. Fill out the remaining notes with crotchets, using the degrees of the scale marked under the stave.

a.)

Keynote   3rd   5th   4th   7th   6th   5th   3rd

b.)

Keynote   3rd   5th   4th   6th   5th   3rd   2nd

c.)

Keynote   2nd   4th   3rd   2nd   5th   2nd   6th

d.)

Keynote Keynote 7th   5th   3rd   4th   2nd   6th

A fanfare is a short piece of music usually played by a loud, brassy instrument like a trumpet. Since ancient times fanfares have been used to announce that an important person has entered a room, like a President or a Queen.

4. Name the key and degrees of the scale that are marked with a star in these brassy fanfares. Write your answers underneath the noteheads.

Key:_____

Key:_____

TONIC TRIADS

Here are three degrees of the scale that sound great when played together at the same time. When more than two notes are played at the same time, we call it a **CHORD**.

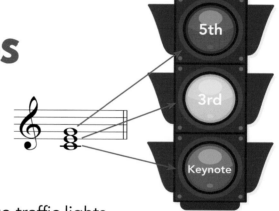

The three notes are stacked on top of each other, a bit like traffic lights.

A **tri**cycle has three wheels, a **tri**angle has three sides, and a **tri**ceratops has three horns.

Let's look at our chord again.

Because our chord has three notes, we call it a **TRIAD**.

Another word for the keynote is the **TONIC**.

This chord is a **TONIC TRIAD** because it has the tonic note at the bottom. It also contains the third and fifth degrees of the scale. A tonic triad always contains these degrees of the scale.

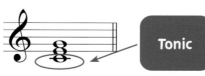

WOAH! That is a lot of new vocabulary.

And breathe.

You may want to run around and scream a bit, now. Or have a cool glass of water. Or perhaps go for a gentle walk.

Feeling better? Let's go back over those words together. Match up the words to the correct definition with a line.

Degrees of the scale	Another word for "keynote."
Keynote	More than two notes sounding simultaneously.
Chord	The most important note in a scale, after which the scale is named.
Triad	The numbers assigned to each note of a scale according to its chronological order.
Tonic	A specific type of chord containing three notes.

Here are the tonic triads in all the keys that we know. (Remember, every triad stacks the tonic, third degree, and fifth degree of the scale.)

C Major   G Major   D Major   F Major

5. Write the tonic triads out again in the bass clef, below. Don't forget the key signature.

C Major   G Major   D Major   F Major

6. Add the other note names to these traffic-light triads to form a tonic triad.

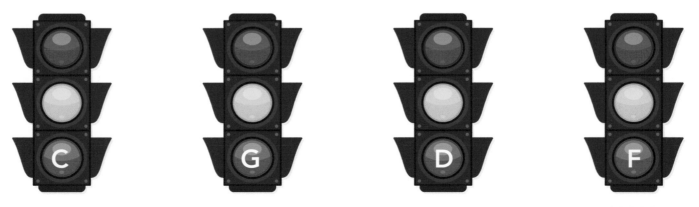

7. Finish this triceratops fanfare using only the notes of the D major tonic triad. You can use any rhythm you want but make sure you have the correct number of beats in each bar. End on the tonic to make the fanfare sound complete.

INTERVALS

Not that kind of interval! A musical *INTERVAL* is the distance between two notes. Each interval has its own special sound.

A *HARMONIC INTERVAL* is when the notes sound together. A *MELODIC INTERVAL* is when the notes are played directly one after another.

Interval Name	Harmonic Interval	Melodic Interval	Sounds Like
2nd			2nds sound close together and crunchy. You can almost hear the notes fighting!
3rd			3rds sound beautiful. The two notes get along like the best of friends.
4th			4ths and 5ths sound strong and pure. Composers loved to use them in the medieval age. They still sound like a brave knight ready for battle.
5th			
6th			6ths also sound beautiful, just like 3rds but a bit more open-sounding and light.
7th			7ths sound a bit uncomfortable. You can almost hear the top note reaching up. They often sound a bit sad, too.
Octave			Octaves are the purest of all! The notes sound similar even though they're eight notes apart.

IMPORTANT!

You calculate an interval by counting from the bottom note to the top note. (When you count, you always include the note you start on as the number "1").

So, C–E is a 3rd: C ("1")–D ("2")–E ("3").

8. Here are some different keynotes. Write the second note that makes the melodic interval described below. Write your note as a crotchet, **higher** than the note given.

| 2nd | 5th | 3rd | Octave |

| 6th | 4th | 7th | 3rd |

9. Use an arrow to match the harmonic interval to the description.

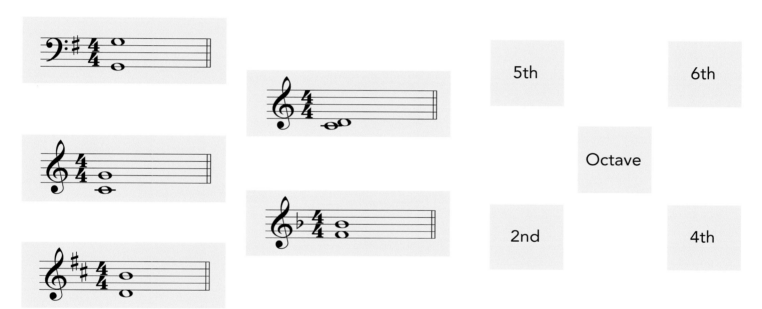

5th   6th

Octave

2nd   4th

10. It's time to play everyone's second-favourite game show!*

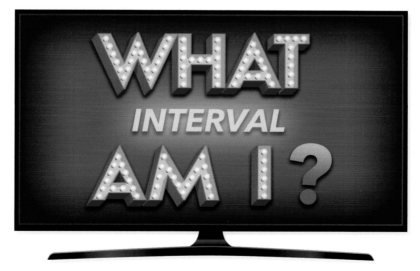

a.) I am a close, crunchy interval. You can hear my notes fighting together!   _____

b.) I am a beautiful interval (even if I say so myself), and bigger than a 5th.   _____

c.) I am a strong and pure interval but I'm not a 5th.   _____

d.) I am the purest interval of them all!   _____   *Still no prizes, I'm afraid.

Here's a fanfare that the school used to have in their music cupboard… until Dotty the dog ate it.

D.S. al Fine means go back to the symbol 𝄋 and play until you see the word "Fine," (which just means "the end").

We can think about reading sheet music containing this sign as like a map, plotting a journey.

- Cecil is walking home from orchestra rehearsal.
- He gets to D.S. al Fine and realises he dropped his flute at the 𝄋 sign.
- So, Cecil has to go all the way back to 𝄋 in order to get his flute.
- At last, Cecil can now carry on home, which is at "Fine."

11. a.) On the stave, write in the names of the melodic intervals indicated by brackets.

   b.) Circle the bar that contains all three notes of the F major tonic triad.

YOU BE THE COMPOSER!

The crowd have arrived in their swimming gear. The Mayor is on his way, so it's time to compose your fanfare!

Write it in G major, lasting eight bars. Use lots of notes in the tonic triad and strong-sounding intervals like 4ths and 5ths. Your fanfare will sound solid if you start and end on the tonic note. Then, why not try playing it on your instrument or asking someone to do it for you?

COMPOSE YOURSELF

Another composer who really made a splash was the musician Julia Perry. She wrote music in the twentieth century after studying in Europe with some of the finest teachers. Even though she was paralysed on the right side of her body later in life, she practised writing with her left hand until she was able to use it to carry on composing! Now, that's resilience. Have a listen to some of her music; Perry's *Prelude* for piano is both warm and very cool. (Go figure that one out!)

WHAT'S A GOLFER'S FAVOURITE STYLE OF MUSIC?

DAD JOKE CORNER

SWING MUSIC!

HOW DO I FEEL?

In this chapter, we learnt all about *DEGREES OF THE SCALE*, *TONIC TRIADS*, and *INTERVALS*. How do you think it went?

Yes, I understand all of this.	🙂	Try expanding your fanfare so it lasts 16 bars.
I think I understand but some bits were tricky.	😐	Great job for realising this. Look through the notes again and ask your teacher about the tricky bits.
I still don't understand most of it.	☹️	Hey, all of us struggle sometimes. Go over from the beginning with your teacher or another adult. To get some extra help, download more worksheet exercises, here. 

MY THEORY SCRAPBOOK

Chord: Three or more notes sounded simultaneously.

Degrees of the Scale: The numbers assigned to each note of a scale according to its chronological order. (In C major, "D" is the second degree of the scale.)

D.S. al Fine: A symbol in sheet music meaning to go back to the symbol 𝄋 and play until you see the word "Fine."

Fanfare: A short, triumphant piece of music played by brass instruments. Usually to announce an important person, event, or occasion.

Harmonic Interval: The gap between two notes played simultaneously. You can calculate an interval by counting from one note to another. (You must include the note you start on as "1.")

Keynote: The most important note in a scale, after which the scale is named. (See also "Tonic.")

Melodic Interval: The gap between notes played consecutively. You can calculate an interval by counting from one note to another. (You must include the note you start on as "1.")

Tonic: The most important note in a scale, after which the scale is named. (See also "Keynote.")

Triad: A chord consisting of three notes; each note is stacked a 3rd apart from the last. A "tonic triad" has the tonic at the bottom and contains the third and fifth degrees of the scale on top, in that order.

Gravy: Ghosts' favourite sauce.

WE'VE LEARNT ALL THIS!

Well done, composer! You saved the town from disappointment. Go for a swim, you deserve it!

You've also completed the whole of *MUSIC THEORY FOR KIDS*! Let's remember what we've learnt. Tick the yellow box if you think you understand the topic. If you're not sure, speak to a teacher and do some extra worksheets, which are available online.

RHYTHM

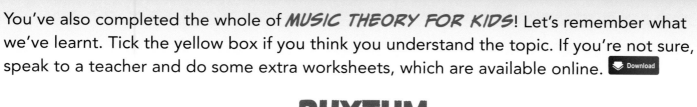

| 4 beats | 3 beats | 2 beats | 1+1/2 beats | 1 beat | 3/4 beat | 1/2 beat | 1/4 beat |

I KNOW THE VALUE OF ALL THESE NOTES.

| 4 beats (or the whole bar) | 2 beats | 1 beat | 1/2 beat | 1/4 beat |

I KNOW THE VALUE OF ALL THESE RESTS.

$\frac{4}{4}$ $\frac{3}{4}$ $\frac{2}{4}$

I KNOW WHAT THESE TIME SIGNATURES MEAN.

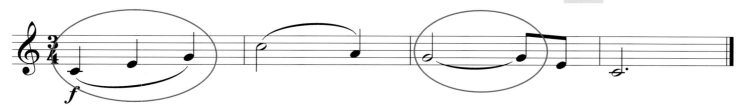

A **slur** means moving smoothly between two or more notes of different pitches.

A **tie** adds the values of two notes together. A tie is between two notes of the same pitch.

I KNOW THE DIFFERENCE BETWEEN THESE TWO CURVED LINES.

I KNOW HOW TO GROUP NOTES TOGETHER CORRECTLY WITH BEAMS.

PITCH

I KNOW THE NAMES OF ALL THESE NOTES AND SYMBOLS.

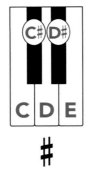

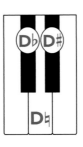

A sharp raises a note by a semitone.

A flat lowers a note by a semitone.

A natural cancels out a sharp or a flat.

I KNOW THE NAMES OF ALL THESE SYMBOLS AND WHAT THEY DO.

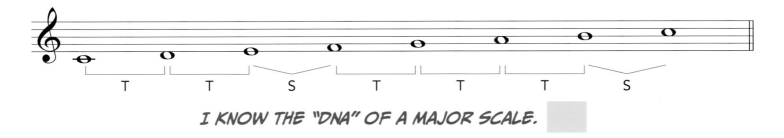

I KNOW THE "DNA" OF A MAJOR SCALE.

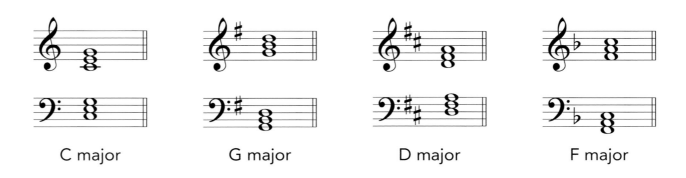

C major   G major   D major   F major

I KNOW THE KEY SIGNATURES AND TONIC TRIADS OF THESE KEYS.

2nd 3rd 4th 5th

6th 7th Octave

I KNOW THE NAMES OF ALL THESE INTERVALS.

Italian Word	English Word	Musical Symbol
Forte	Loud	$\boldsymbol{f}$
Fortissimo	Very Loud	$\boldsymbol{ff}$
Mezzo Forte	Moderately Loud	$\boldsymbol{mf}$
Mezzo Piano	Moderately Soft	$\boldsymbol{mp}$
Piano	Soft	$\boldsymbol{p}$
Pianissimo	Very Soft	$\boldsymbol{pp}$
Crescendo (*cresc.*)	Gradually Getting Louder	<
Diminuendo (*dim.*)	Gradually Getting Softer	>
Decrescendo (*decresc.*)	Gradually Getting Softer	>

Italian Word	English Word
Adagio	Slow
Lento	Slow
Andante	At a Walking Speed
Moderato	Moderately
Allegretto	Fairly Fast
Allegro	Fast and Lively
Rallentando (*rall.*)	Gradually Getting Slower
Ritardando (*rit.*)	Gradually Getting Slower
Ritenuto (*rit.*)	Held Back
Accelerando (*accel.*)	Gradually Getting Faster
Cantabile	In a Singing Style
Poco	A Little
Mezzo	Half/Medium/Somewhat
Dal Segno / D.S. al Fine	Repeat from the Sign up to "Fine"

I KNOW THE MEANING OF ALL THESE MUSICAL EXPRESSIONS.

Cecil Smith